INTERNATIONAL FOOTBALL BOOK
No. 17

A pictorial tribute to the giant-killers of 1974–75. Champions Leeds United were held to a draw by Southern League Wimbledon. Above a Wimbledon forward beats goalkeeper Harvey to a cross . . . but the ball goes wide.

INTERNATIONAL FOOTBALL BOOK

No. 17

Edited by Eric Batty

with contributions by

PAUL BREITNER	BILLY BONDS	DENIS TUEART
DAVE THOMAS	BERTI VOGTS	DAVE WATSON
BOB LATCHFORD	BARRY HULSHOFF	RAY CLEMENCE
PAUL MADELEY	MARTIN BUCHAN	BRIAN GLANVILLE

SOUVENIR PRESS LTD LONDON

Distributed by
SPORTSHELF
P. O. Box 634
New Rochelle, N. Y. 10802

ISBN 0 285 62210 2

Filmset by Keyspools Limited, Golborne, Lancashire
Printed in Great Britain by
Redwood Burn Limited, Trowbridge & Esher

CONTENTS

6

LIST OF ILLUSTRATIONS

WEST HAM ARE MORE COMPETITIVE NOW

says Hammers' Captain
BILLY BONDS

Billy Bonds in a tussle with Alan Birchenall (Leicester City).

AS LONG as I have been associated with West Ham they've had a reputation for playing attractive, entertaining football and in my time we've had some very good sides.

When I arrived from Charlton Athletic in May, 1967, the team had already made its mark, winning the FA Cup and the European Cup Winners Cup, and was in the process of rebuilding. I was a bit over-awed at first, playing with World Cup stars like Bobby Moore, Geoff Hurst and Martin Peters, but within a couple of games I felt more or less at home.

Almost immediately we went abroad on tour and then before the start of the 1967–68 season we went to play on the continent again. I realised very quickly that though they were exceptional players, they were also what I would call 'normal blokes'.

Since then we've maintained the club's reputation for good football and come close to honours several times. Until last season, perhaps the side we had around 1972 was the best. I really thought we had chances in the 1971–72 League Cup, specially after we beat Stoke City 2–1 away in the first leg of the semi-final. But that tie went to four games, ending in Manchester where Bobby Ferguson was badly injured and Bobby Moore had to go in goal for a spell.

The following season we had a really good spell after Christmas and finished with the highest number of points the club had ever earned in the First Division. We had 'Pop' Robson and Ted McDougall scoring goals and were still playing our usual flowing football. Many people thought we were going to win the league in 1973–74 but somehow it all went wrong and we finished up struggling to avoid relegation. I still don't understand how that happened because I really thought at the start of that season that we could have won the league.

Our style of play hasn't changed and we still set out to entertain at home or away. Other sides come to play us at Upton Park with a really defensive attitude, but we never put the result before the game as some others do.

We've always tried to get results but until last season we seemed unable to hit on the perfect marriage–playing entertaining football and getting consistently good results.

The squad we've got now is probably the best I've known at West Ham. In the past, we seldom had

Ted McDougall (above) looked good and scored goals in 1972–73 season for West Ham but failed inexplicably in the following season and moved on to Norwich City.

Bobby Moore (above) captain of West Ham and England when Bonds arrived from Charlton. 'Just a normal bloke' says Bonds.

much depth in reserve and one or two injuries created problems at critical times. But now we have a very good team and a good squad in depth, so much so, that at times it's difficult to name our best side.

West Ham as a team have also become more competitive. The forwards chase back when our attacks break down and above all we compete where it hurts sometimes–in the opponents penalty area.

We've become more competitive in defence too, but let me emphasise that this doesn't mean we've become tougher or dirty. All we've done is to deny space to our opponents, we close people up and don't give them room to play. We win the ball fairly and having won it, we try to attack in an entertaining way.

Perhaps our failure in the past has been that we were not successful at getting the ball. Once we had it, we showed all our skill and attacking flair, but we didn't have as much of the ball as we now because we didn't compete enough for it.

Now we get plenty of the ball and with players like Trevor Brooking and Graham Paddon we have plenty of what the critics call flair. Brooking is very graceful, skilful and intelligent, and when he's on song, he's the best in England. Paddon also is a very good attacking player with an elegant left foot. He pings the ball about, bending and curling his passes just as he wants–and he works too.

Ron Greenwood set the pattern of West Ham's play, always seeking perfection in football with players who have a high degree of individual skill

Billy Jennings (left) is one of the players who have added a more competitive edge to West Ham's play, seen here helping in defence at a corner kick. Above, Frank Lampard who was capped for England two years ago.

but also think a lot about the game. John Lyall has much in common with him, but the big difference that comes across from John is that he doesn't like losing. This is no reflection on Mr. Greenwood who I'm sure wanted to win everything, but he just didn't seem to let it show so much.

We didn't see much of Mr. Greenwood last season but I'm sure he worked very closely with Mr. Lyall behind the scenes. Between them they've produced a new, more competitive West Ham without losing any of the elegant skills. Our philosophy now, I

*Billy Bonds (above right) slams home a penalty and (left) Trevor Brooking in action,
'the best in England when he's on song'.*

would say is . . . 'if we match the opposition for effort and workrate, then our skill will come out on top'.

Our training hasn't changed much since Mr. Greenwood slipped out of the limelight. We still do most of our training with the ball and I know my skill has improved considerably as a result of it all.

But if I'm more skilful now than when I first arrived, my attitude to the game hasn't changed. I used to fly about with Charlton, a right back in those days when George Cohen was dashing up the wing for England.

I always hoped to play for England and was very optimistic when I played twice for the England Under 23 team. But after that I switched to play in midfield and I don't think that helped my chances.

One day I remember Martin Peters said, 'be careful you don't cut your own throat and find yourself out of the team' soon after Ron Greenwood moved me to right half. I didn't think much about it at the time but on reflection, I think it would have improved my England chances if I'd stayed a right-back.

Don't misunderstand me, I've never regretted becoming a midfield player because being involved in the game all the time suits my temperament. I also enjoy scoring goals and as a midfield player I've knocked in quite a few. I also take penalties now—but though I've scored with most of them, I still wouldn't say I like taking them. But it just happened. 'Pop' Robson used to take them but after missing one, he didn't want to take the next one we got . . . and I took it–and kept the job.

Being realistic, I'm 28 now and I can't see myself getting the chance to establish myself in the England team. I could still conceivably get the odd cap, but if I was to become a regular I think I would have got the chance earlier. I'd jump at the chance of course, but I think it's too late for me now.

But we have other players at West Ham, Brooking and Paddon in particular who I feel should be in the England side. Frank Lampard did get a cap two years ago, but he's a far better player now than he was then yet seems to have been overlooked.

Mervyn Day's chance will surely come and Kevin Lock has improved enormously. He was always very skilful but he improved in every way last season, winning the ball consistently now, which used to be a failing.

I find it difficult to understand how England chances don't seem to come to West Ham players any more. It isn't only my opinion either, for up and down the country, wherever I go, people seem to agree that West Ham are the best football side in the country.

With this overwhelming view, it would seem logical that one or two West Ham players should be in the England team.

Graham Paddon (below) one of the West Ham players Bonds thinks should get an England chance. 'An elegant left foot and a hard worker, he pings the ball about curling and bending his passes just as he wants.'

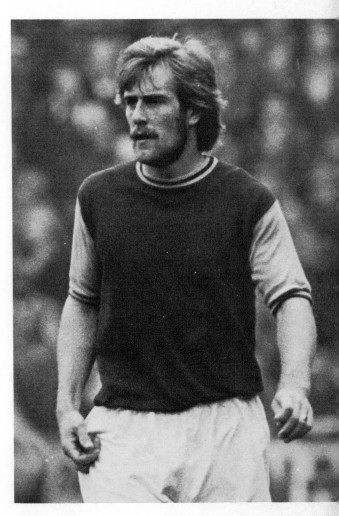

MANCHESTER UNITED STAR MARTI

WRITES ABOUT

THE BLACK DAY A

UCHAN

HAMPDEN PARK

▲ ▼ ▲

WEDNESDAY, 14th February, 1973, was the day I thought my brief career as a Scotland player was over. England beat Scotland 5–0 that evening, on an icy pitch at Hampden Park and I was one of several players discarded. New manager Willie Ormond clearly had to do something after a defeat like that and decided to rebuild the team he had inherited from Tommy Docherty, who had moved on to take command of Manchester United.

Ormond's rebuilt side went on to finish the job Docherty had started, beating Czechoslovakia 2–1 in Glasgow to qualify for the final stages of the World Cup. By that time I was resigned to spending the summer of 1974 doing odd jobs around the house and working in the garden.

On the left Martin Buchan, left half or sweeper in action clearing spectacularly from the goalmouth and (right) a recent portrait.

Then, right out of the blue, I was called back into the Scottish squad for a friendly match with West Germany, only four months before the big competition got under way. George Connelly of Celtic had just suffered a broken ankle and with several other players unavailable for various reasons, I got an unexpected opportunity to re-establish myself at international level.

The game was played in the Wald Stadion in Frankfurt, where we later met Brazil and Yugoslavia in the World Cup. I was given the job of marking Gerd Müller and though we lost 2–1, it

Willie Ormond (left), Scotland team manager who recalled Martin Buchan and finished the job started by Tommy Docherty. Below, George Connelly (on left) in action for Celtic, who broke an ankle to let Buchan regain his place.

Gerd Müller (on left above) and Uli Hoeness his Bayern clubmate who have a very good understanding.

was some consolation for me that he did not score.

Müller was extremely quick, much quicker than I had imagined from seeing clips of him in action on television. He had a very good understanding with with his club colleagues Uli Hoeness and Franz Beckenbauer, and I found he tried to draw me away from goal, into false positions where defenders would not normally like to go–confident that his speed would enable him to be first back into the gaps created, to reach balls played in by Beckenbauer & Co.

I was optimistic about my chances after that and presumably Mr. Ormond was satisfied too for looking back, this was almost certainly the game that enabled me to achieve an ambition that I thought beyond my reach: to play for Scotland in the World Cup finals.

Billy Bremner, Scotland's captain, with Wilson Piazza (Brazil) before the 0–0 draw (far page, top). Martin Buchan (below left) clears from a Leeds United attack. This page (left) Brazil's 1970 World Cup star Jairzinho who, says Buchan, was not as good in the 1974 competition as he was in Brazil's Mini-Cup of 1972. Below (this page), Buchan's Manchester United colleague Jim Holton, who, says Martin Buchan, 'confounded even his most severe critics with his displays in Germany duwing the last World Cup.'

John Blackley of Hibernians was preferred to me for the first match against Zaire which was won 2–0 and then I got back into the side for the two drawn games against Brazil and Yugoslavia. I had previously played against both countries in the Mini-Mundial staged in Brazil in 1972, so I knew a little about them.

For most of the Brazil match my immediate opponent was Jairzinho, but he wasn't the player he had been two years previously. Neither for that matter was Rivelino. But bearing in mind that players of the calibre of Pele, Gerson and Tostao are virtually irreplacable, I think Brazil did well to reach the play-off for third place.

The 0–0 draw with Brazil was followed by a 1–1 result against Yugoslavia which meant that although unbeaten, we didn't qualify for the second stage.

featured the two teams that had impressed me most in the competition. I had always fancied the West Germans, playing in their own country. But when Johan Cruyff produced that devastating run in the first minute to be brought down for a penalty, I thought I might be proved wrong. In the end however, it was my favourite player Franz Beckenbauer who received the trophy.

Much as I admired the Dutch side, I felt that the Germans had the edge in experience, home advantage, and above all, they had just as many, if not more, outstanding players in the positions that mattered.

Bobby Clark, my former colleague at Aberdeen, reminded me recently that several of the Dutch

Johan Neeskens (left) the Dutch World Cup star who played in the 1970 UEFA Youth Tournament in Scotland, and (below) Wolfgang Overath, a player Buchan has long admired.

Why did we fail? We simply didn't score enough goals. Perhaps we were unfortunate to meet Zaire first, compared to Brazil who knew what they had to do and just managed to beat them 3–0.

Zaire were defensively naive at times, but they played with a great deal of spirit and not a little skill. Had we met them later, when they were perhaps feeling the strain physically, it might have been different. But in the final analysis our 2–0 win was not enough to see us through to the quarter final stages.

The Scottish squad flew back to Glasgow two days after the game against Yugoslavia to a wonderful reception from a Scottish crowd who obviously felt we had acquitted ourselves well.

I watched the final at home on television and it

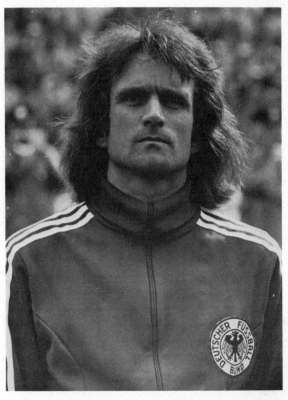

Martin Buchan's favourite player, Franz Beckenbauer, who received the World Cup (left).

squad, including Johan Neeskens had participated in the UEFA Youth Tournament held in Scotland in 1970, so perhaps Holland's chance will come again in 1978.

Each World Cup brings outstanding players to our notice. My pick of the crop would be Cruyff and Neeskens from Holland; Wolfgang Overath, a player for whom I have a great admiration, and of course Franz Beckenbauer. The performance of Lobilo, Africa's Footballer of the Year, for Zaire against Scotland, also impressed me.

For Scotland, Sandy Jardine underlined that as an attacking full back, he is the equal of anyone currently playing international football. I was also pleased to see my Manchester United club-mate, Jim Holton, confound even his most severe critics with his displays in Germany.

There are other individuals worthy of note but the World Cup is, after all, a competition in which we expect to see the best 16 teams in the world. But did we?

England's failure to play in Germany was disappointing. They failed to qualify because they couldn't convert scoring chances into goals, which was the same reason for unbeaten Scotland's early return home. England of course, have appointed a new manager to give them a new approach but my personal feeling is that the game at club level will

have to become more adventurous before we see an appreciable improvement at international level.

There are sides in Britain who attempt to combine organisation with entertaining, attacking play, but they are in the minority. The general level of skill has improved, but only time will tell whether more clubs will encourage that skill to be seen more often.

I suppose it could be argued that I have played a part in denying players with skill, the opportunity to exhibit it. I've been sent out to mark particular opponents closely, notably Gerd Müller.

Outstanding players have always been singled out for special attention and always will be. If I would prefer to play a more free role, it would be untrue if I failed to say that I didn't derive some satisfaction from preventing one of the world's most prolific goalscorers from scoring against my team.

Europe's international teams are now playing for places in the final stages of the 1976 European Nations Cup. We really needed a win against Spain, in Valencia, where the atmosphere was quite intense. The result turned on a situation in the Scottish goalmouth in which I handled the ball on the line. Even after seeing numerous replays of the incident, I'm not sure whether the ball did cross the line.

In any event, the referee awarded a goal, denying us the possibility, however remote, of our goal-keeper, David Harvey, saving the penalty kick that most of my colleagues thought should have been awarded. Now we have to depend on other teams in our section to get results that will keep our slim hopes alive.

My international experiences have I think, made me a more confident player at club level and also helped to ease the disappointment of United's relegation.

But before I'm ready to live with my memories of 1974, I am still young enough, if selected to play in the 1978 World Cup and even in 1982. I expect England and West Germany to be among the favourites next time, but having tasted blood in 1974, I see no reason why Scotland shouldn't qualify again . . . and even do better in the finals.

Scotland right back Sandy Jardine, 'the equal of any attacking full back in the international arena' says Martin Buchan.

*The world's ace footballer—Johan Cruyff of Holland and CF Barcelona who made th.
number 14 famous. Above (left and right) in World Cup action and below (left and right)
playing for Barcelona against their neighbours RCD Espanol.*

THE BEST FOOTBALL TEAMS
DO NOT ALWAYS
THE W

VIN
RLD CUP

By
BERTI VOGTS
**right back of
West Germany
and
Borussia Mönchengladbach**

Berti Vogts (above right) suggests Holland were the best 'football' team in the World Cup. Left, Franz Beckenbauer holds the trophy aloft, applauded by colleagues Maier and Breitner.

IT IS an unfortunate fact of football life that very often, the team that plays the best football does not always win the World Cup. It happened that way in 1966, when Portugal finished up in third place and the same was true in 1970.

In the Mexico competition most experts thought West Germany was the best team in the series, but we lost 4–3 to Italy in an incredibly exciting semi-final, and it happened to Holland last year.

It is possible that we had easier opponents in the earlier matches but whatever the reason, I feel we won because we had more fighting power and will to win.

Over the last few years, West German football has been through a period of tremendous success but we must be careful not to become complacent. If that happens, we will lose out, because the international game is developing fast.

Some people have suggested that the West German team that won the 1972 European Championship was better than the 1974 side. My own view is that in 1972 we played some brilliant football in a modern style, but in the World Cup we had more fighting spirit and will to win. Clearly, the ideal would be a combination of both and it is along these lines that I think football will progress in the next few years.

Obviously the decision of some of our players to withdraw from international football has created problems. Personally, I would never pass up the chance to play for the national team as long as the manager feels I will be useful. But I must emphasise that this is not an implied criticism of some of my former colleagues.

I would never attempt to pass judgement on players that decline to play when they can still play a very important role in the national team. This is because there may well be reasons for their decisions that I am not aware of. Nevertheless, I do feel it is too bad that some players care very little whether or not they are playing in the national team.

But having said that it does seem to me that some players have their sense of values mixed up. Having won almost every honour open to them and made a lot of money, they seem to have lost all ambition and need to start re-thinking. In football, the willingness to work and enthusiasm for the battle is vitally important–if players and teams are to stay on top. Otherwise it is very easy to become a second class player.

For myself, I am still full of ambition. Before the 1974 World Cup I had already helped my club win two Bundesliga championships, but I would still like to do it again very much . . . and win the UEFA Cup. Then having earned a place in the European Cup, I'd like to help win that too.

The temptations of playing abroad, particularly in Spain, are obvious. For one thing, a good player can make twice as much money in Spain, and on top of that the taxes are very much lower than in Germany. From a playing point of view, it is also easier in Spain compared to the Bundesliga or the English First Division. But I have no desire to play in Spain.

I started my career with Borussia, and my contract still has three years to run before it expires

Berti Vogts in action for West Germany (right) and lower left, an anxious moment for the Germans in their narrow 1–0 World Cup win over Poland.

Borussia have two young players with the skills of Netzer and Beckenbauer, on left is Christian Kulik and (above) the 'new Beckenbauer' Uli Stielike in action.

and I plan to end my playing days with them.

For several years I played with Gunter Netzer for Borussia, before he went to Real Madrid. I have no doubt that he and Franz Beckenbauer are the two most outstanding players I have been associated with. These two are players of real genius and playing with them is the ultimate experience in football.

Since Netzer went to Spain we have missed his organising ability at Borussia, particularly in home games in which the visitors play with a packed defence. I think both sides now regret the decision to part company that they made in 1973.

I was always a great admirer of Netzer and at the time when his contract with Borussia was ending, I fought like a lion to keep him with us. So much so that it created some unpleasantness between myself and our Board of Directors, though that has long been forgotten.

The style of Borussia is the creation of our coach Hennes Weisweiler. He discovers the players and builds them up, developing their ability and creating self-confidence. He is always ready with encouragement when players hit a bad patch and need uplifting.

Dietmar Danner, who played for Germany in 1973 is one of our brightest young players. He went through a crisis period last season but he is exceptionally gifted and I am sure he will re-assert himself.

We have two other young players that are probably unknown in England who I am sure are going to become real stars–Uli Stielike and Christian Kulik.

Stielike's talents are quite outstanding, the most gifted player since Gunter Netzer. I am sure he will ultimately replace Franz Beckenbauer in the national team.

Kulik really came on very strongly last season and as the midfield general, he has in his own way, become a personality within the team. But Borussia's style is above all collective, we play as a team and we shall all help them both to develop their talents to the full.

Borussia's football is a reflection of Hennes Weisweiler who believes fanatically in the British style of play. His aim was to combine the traditional English attributes: speed, fighting power and offensive spirit with the German technical ability.

I also have a very high regard for English football. When I end my career as a player, I plan to spend two months studying English training methods and then as things stand now, I hope to become the coach of the German Youth team.

Leeds and Liverpool have been the most consistent English teams in recent years. But the sides that have impressed me most when I have played against them were Liverpool and Everton. And my favourite team was always Manchester United.

In my estimation, there is no need for drastic changes in the English game though there would perhaps be an improvement if the English clubs were to adopt some of the more progressive ideas from continental football.

It is too bad that England's international prestige is not very high at the moment, but these things go in cycles. The English national team is now in the process of rebuilding, but I am sure they will come again. Every country reaches a low point at certain intervals, but the stronger soccer countries usually bounce back even stronger than they were before.

The important thing I believe, is for players to enjoy their football, as I do. I have played full back on both flanks and even as a libero or sweeper. Naturally I like to play full back, preferably on the right, because there you can go forward a little more. But often I am given a tight-marking role as I was in the 1974 World Cup Final, marking Johan Cruyff.

Marking Cruyff was one of the most challenging tasks I have been given because he is so unpredictable and very skilful, as well as quick. I accept these special assignments because as a professional it is something one must do, but being honest, I enjoy playing defensively against really good players.

It is always a battle of wits and skill and I enjoy the challenge. And assessing myself objectively, the defensive aspect of the game is where my special talents lie.

Vogts in action in the 1974 World Cup Final, challenging Johan Cruyff whom he shut out of the game.

EVERTON'S BOB LATCHFORD

SAYS

'WE ARE NOT NEGATIVE AT GOODISON'

EVERTON have always had a reputation for good football–which means attacking football–and that was one of the reasons that made me want to join them when Birmingham City put me up for transfer.

But last season, after three or four years in the doldrums, when we first began to shape up as possible champions, the knockers started to criticise us for what they called defensive tactics.

It just isn't true and I would point out that for most of last season we were scoring more goals away from home than anyone else. And away from home is where most teams play defensively if they are going to do it at all.

Our alleged, negative approach was first highlighted after the Spurs manager, Terry Neil, slated us after we played at Tottenham and it slowly built up from there.

Looking at a game like football logically, you have to recognise that there will be times when the other side has the ball and they can stay on top for lengthy periods. Our aim is to attack and score goals, which is certainly what I am in the side for, but before we can attack, we must regain possession

A recent portrait of Bob Latchford . . . right.

of the ball. To do that when the other side is attacking there is no alternative but to drop back and try to win it.

This applies equally to every side in the league. We only adopt a defensive posture when we have to . . . and when we get the ball we use it to launch an attack on the enemy goal. Anyone who thinks any side can attack all afternoon is living in cuckoo land.

Many people have asked how it affected my play when I got tagged 'Britain's most expensive player' after my transfer to Everton. The simple truth is that it didn't bother me at all. If you let things like that get on top of you, then you have no chance. Of course it could be a problem if a player with a £300,000 plus price tag went for weeks without

getting a goal, but luckily that didn't happen to me. I just put all thoughts of transfer fees to one side, put on my boots and played.

That is what I am paid for, playing and getting goals and I work hard at it, both in training and in matches. You cannot do less with a club like Everton who have always had a great football tradition and a solid following. When you pull on their blue jersey, something happens that is difficult to explain but you just feel you have to do well for the sake of the club and the fans.

More or less the crowd at Goodison is similar to the St. Andrews crowd when Birmingham City were going well. Both sets of fans are very good and when the club does well it generates a new atmosphere. Liverpool fans have earned a reputation for creating

Bob Latchford is an admirer of the Dutch game. Above Germany put pressure on Holland's goal in the World Cup Final.

an atmosphere both at Anfield and away from home. They are fairly reckoned to be amongst the most discerning and appreciative crowds in the country, but in my book, the crowds at St. Andrews and Goodison are just as well informed about the intricacies of the game, just as appreciative of good football and when their team is successful they create the same kind of atmosphere. In my opinion it is success that creates atmosphere.

Generally, no matter how much noise the fans make it has little effect on the players. Speaking only for myself I am almost impervious to the fans

Photo left shows Martin Dobson, Everton's £300,000 signing from Burnley, leading his colleagues on a training stint with Latchford on the left (Number 2).

during the game. Of course you are aware of spectators, but concentrating on the game, they are just part of the background.

A local derby can be different but that's because the build up to the game which starts several days earlier, makes you aware of the importance of the occasion. Once the game gets under way, the crowd recedes into the background. But having said all that, the noise at a big derby can be deafening and if you do well and the crowd responds it can certainly give the players a big lift.

Since I joined Everton, my style of play has altered quite a bit. At Birmingham I think I was

'Johan Cruyff (above) the number one player today' says Bob Latchford who admits he could never play the way the Dutch star does. 'I just aim to do a good job scoring goals with no frills.'

simply a goal scorer, a finisher of the moves that others built up. But with Everton you seldom see me upfield without support. This is because our manager, Billy Bingham, says the whole side has to stay compact. No one has to be left isolated as an individual.

The result is that I play a more complete role in the team, sharing in the build up in attacking moves and I enjoy being more involved.

The kind of football we are trying to play at Everton is related to the type of game being played by the best sides in Holland like Ajax, FC Twente and Feyenoord. Whether we will be able to match

them for what they call *total football* is a matter of opinion but that's what we are aiming at.

The top Dutch clubs have been well known for their classy football for several seasons and of course their best players showed it all again last summer in the World Cup, but the team I rate most highly of all is the West German side, Borussia Monchengladbach.

Borussia's football is very similar to the Dutch game but very exciting and generally more skilful. It's just that bit different, with more emphasis on skill that is spread equally through the side. Even amongst the back four and the strikers like Heynckes. Whatever his number, all the Borussia players have real skill with the ball.

Of course you cannot escape the fact that the number one player today is Johan Cruyff. Though he too plays at centre forward, I am quite unlike him and could never even hope to play the game his way. Cruyff is tremendously skilful, very quick off the mark with the ball, and in everything he does he seems to me to have a lazy look, probably because he makes it all look so easy.

I remember being impressed by the football in Denmark too when I played there for England's Under 23 team. All the Danes had a high degree of skill that was quite remarkable considering the Danes are all amateurs.

I'm just a straightforward type of player myself which is probably the reason why I admire the more skilful players. I don't try to bend or swerve the ball when I shoot, I just aim to do a good job with no frills. Six foot odd, I have two good feet for shooting and I'm a bit useful in the air. When I get myself into a shooting position, nine times out of ten I just hit the ball hard–hit it with everything I've got. Maybe the tenth time I'll try to place the ball, just

'If there is a key man in the Everton team it is Dave Clements' writes Bob Latchford. Clements (seen in action on the right) 'has an excellent left foot and has the ability to steady them down and make things tick.'

Bob Latchford (right) says his job is to get the ball in the net and nine times out of ten he simply hits the ball with everything he's got. Here he turns away after a shot at goal.

...s a variation, but I never try to mess about being too clever. Just get it in the back of the net is my philosophy.

I work hard at it too in training, mostly inside the penalty box which is where the majority of the chances come in matches. It sounds simple but all I aim to do is go to meet the ball, inside the box, get there first and score—with head or foot.

One thing I rarely do is practice dead ball shooting which isn't really my thing. Above all, I'd never dream of taking penalty kicks. To be a successful penalty taker I believe you have to be

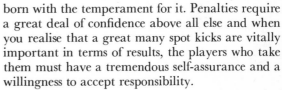

born with the temperament for it. Penalties require a great deal of confidence above all else and when you realise that a great many spot kicks are vitally important in terms of results, the players who take them must have a tremendous self-assurance and a willingness to accept responsibility.

I'll chase balls that I don't have much chance of catching and I'll try a shot from almost any angle in fluid play but I simply wouldn't fancy the job of taking penalties.

Scoring goals is the end product, the result of everyone else's efforts and I accept responsibility of that kind without a thought. But I don't regard myself as the key man in the Everton side. If there is one, I think that distinction belongs to Dave Clements. Dave has an excellent left foot and has the ability to make things tick. When he's on song he steadies the entire team down and despite his skill and his ability to lead and get the best out of other players he's a very powerful player himself.

TOP TWENTY

Another selection of World Stars presented by
BRIAN GLANVILLE

GIANCARLO ANTOGNONI (Fiorentina and Italy) Acclaimed as the second Gianni Rivera, Antognoni, young Perugian, resembled him in precocity and technique, but he is blond where Rivera is dark; and he has a more solid physique. He won his first cap in the difficult match away to Holland in Amsterdam in November, 1974, when he was still only 20: he was born at Marsciano on April 1, 1954. His first club was the little Astimacobi of Division D, in Piedmont, and he made his debut for them at 16. Fiorentina signed him in 1972, giving him his Serie A baptism against Verona in October, 1972, when he was still a mere 18. He was an instant success, impressing everyone with his skill, poise and clever reading of the game; a complete inside-forward. To keep him, Fiorentina, who had bought only a half share from Astimacobi, had to pay a vast fee, but they can hardly regret it. Antognoni's chief problem is that he carries so many of the hopes of an Italian football which has lost much of its self-esteem.

CARLOS BABINGTON (Wattenscheid 09 and Argentina) The blond, curly haired Babington had an outstanding World Cup; the more ironical in that Argentina called him up only when they were already on their European "warming-up" tour. An elegant ball player and splendidly imaginative

things instantly improved. He played in the remaining four matches, scored a fine goal against Sweden, and made the winner in the World Cup Final with his powerful burst on the German right, and cross to Muller. Prior to the tournament, he had made only a few sporadic appearances in the international team. A forceful, enterprising, right sided player with a flair for the important occasion. Born March 29, 1952.

JERZY GORGON (Gornik Zabrze and Poland)

A huge, blond centre-back who successfully played a covering role to Zmuda in the World Cup, having

Carlos Babington (opposite page) and above left, Rainer Bonhof. Below is Jerzy Gorgon the giant stopper from Poland.

passer of the ball, Babington's midfield play at inside-left dominated the match in Stuttgart against Italy. A few years earlier, he would have joined Stoke City, had his father not allowed his British passport to lapse; for he is of English descent. A member of the fine Huracan attack which also included Brindisi and Houseman, he surprisingly moved to a West German Second Division club a few months after the World Cup. Born September 20, 1949.

RAINER BONHOF (Borussia Monchengladbach and West Germany)

After West Germany had lost to East Germany at Hamburg, they called the powerful Bonhof into midfield; and contributed greatly to his team's qualification. Gorgon had already won an Olympic gold medal in 1972, and played for Gornik when they were beaten in the 1970 Cupwinners' Cup Final by Manchester City. Clearly he is seldom beaten in the air, and his reading of the game had improved considerably by the time of the World Cup. Born July 19, 1949.

JEAN-MARC GUILLOU (Angers and France)

It took Guillou seven years to win a regular place in the Angers team; and in 1974, after he had established himself brilliantly in the French national team, he did his best to leave them, staying another year on sufferance. But it is typical of him that he should make that year, a very difficult one for the team, which was much weakened, an outstanding one for selfless, determined play. An extremely elegant player with a delicate touch and splendid distribution, Guillou was first capped in March

René Houseman of Argentina above, and on the left, David Harvey of Leeds United and Scotland.

1974 against Rumania. Early the following season he had a superb match when France beat Poland in Wroclaw. Born at Bouaye on December 20, 1945.

DAVID HARVEY (Leeds United and Scotland)

Scotland's admirable World Cup goalkeeper in 1974, Harvey had already won a Championship medal for Leeds. His goalkeeping had done a vast amount to make their success possible. He had displaced Gary Sprake in the Leeds goal, capable of saves just as brilliant, and immensely more consistent. Harvey is a Leeds man who has spent his whole career with the club; he qualifies for Scotland because his father is a Scot. Has played two Cup Finals for Leeds; winning against Arsenal in 1972, losing a year later against Sunderland.

RONNIE HELLSTROEM (Kaiserslautern and Sweden) By the time the 1974 World Cup was over, Hellstroem, at £30,000, looked a bargain indeed for Kaiserslautern, and must himself have regretted signing his contract before, rather than after the tournament. He played magnificently for the Swedes, his courage and resilience doing much to take them into the second stage. It was a much more satisfactory World Cup for him than 1970's, when an unlucky mistake gave Italy a goal and victory. Born February 21, 1949, he has won over 40 caps for Sweden, and previously played for the Hammarby club.

RENÉ HOUSEMAN (Huracan and Argentina) One of the revelations of the 1974 World Cup, not least with his superb performance and fine goal against Italy in Stuttgart. A tiny but courageous figure, very fast, very incisive, with exceptional ball control, he was only 20 at the time, having emerged in the Huracan club attack. Indeed, his understanding that evening with Babington was quite remarkable. Born July 19, 1953.

WIM JANSEN (Feyenoord and Holland) Though he gave away the penalty from which West Germany equalised in the Final, small, fair haired Jansen had an excellent World Cup. There seemed little chance that he would play till Hulshoff and Muhren dropped out, but he took his chance admirably, having already helped Feyenoord to

Henryk Kasperczak (below) and on the left, Wim Jansen of Feyenoord and Holland.

win the UEFA Cup. A quick, energetic, decisive player, versatile in the manner of the traditional wing-half, he was born on October 28, 1946. Joined Feyenoord when he was ten.

JAN JONGBLOED (FC Amsterdam and Holland) There was something of the fairy tale about Jongbloed's success in the 1974 World Cup. He was 33 years old, he had made but one, truncated appearance, years before, for Holland. It was believed, by Jongbloed as much as anybody, that he had come for the ride; largely to raise morale with his cheerful ways. He had even brought his fishing rods. But injury to Schrijvers put him in the team, and the wisdom of his manager Rinus Michels in choosing him became plain; for Jongbloed's daring, sometimes rash, sorties out of goal were just what was needed by an adventurous team playing a risky offside game. So it was that he helped them materially on their way to the World Cup Final. The following season, he and the veterans of the Amsterdam defence helped the club to a fine run in the UEFA Cup. Born November 25, 1940.

HENRYK KASPERCZAK (Stal Mielec and Poland) Invaluable right hand to the splendid Deyna in Poland's 1974 World Cup midfield, Kasperczak had an excellent tournament; an attacking right-half of skill, constructive and pro-pulsive ability. Made a name for himself helping his club to win the Polish Championship; was capped for the first time against the United States in March, 1972. Born July 10, 1946.

DUNCAN McKENZIE (Leeds United) One of the great successes of the 1974-75 season; after a difficult and controversial beginning. Born in Grimsby, he went to grammar school, joined Nottingham Forest, and sturdily refused to change his individual style for the wall-passing demanded of him. Twice he was farmed out to Mansfield Town, twice recalled. In season 1973-74 he was the star of Forest's fine Cup run, in the summer he went on the England tour as a reserve, came back, demanded a transfer, and was finally bought by Brian Clough for Leeds. Clough went, McKenzie remained, and fought his way into the team; a player of great skill, unusual initiative, an exception-

ally quick turn. His throwing and high jumping characterise the all round athlete.

BJORN NORDQVIST (PSV Eindhoven and Sweden) This veteran stopper had a splendid 1974 World Cup, when he brought the total of his caps to 77, and emerged as one of the best defenders in the tournament. He also played two games for them in Mexico in the 1970 competition. A tall, calm, sturdy player, solid alike in the air and on the ground, he now plays with his compatriot, Edström, for the Dutch team PSV. His original club was IFK Norkopping, which produced the Nordahl brothers of the 1950's. Born October 6, 1942.

BRANKO OBLAK (Hajduk and Yugoslavia) It was a great pity that, late in 1974, a serious tendon injury should put Oblak out of football for many months; it had till then been an outstanding year for him. This strong, compact, blond midfield player with a stupendous shot–the left footer with which he scored against England in Belgrade in May, 1974 was remarkable–had moved with equal success up into the firing line. Born on May 27, 1947, he has won more than thirty caps, and was an outstanding member of the Yugoslav team which first qualified then distinguished itself in the 1974 World Cup.

LAURENT POKOU (Rennes and Ivory Coast) Early in 1974, Rennes at last became the envy of other French clubs by persuading this splendid centre-forward to leave Africa, Abidjan and join them. Twice top scorer in the African Nations Cup, Pokou is a complete player. Ball at his foot, he attacks and beats the opposition; but he is also a maker of goals for other players. He was an instant success when he came to Rennes from Asec Abidjan. He was born in Abidjan on August 10, 1947.

Duncan McKenzie (upper left), Branko Oblak (lower left), Robbie Rensenbrink (above right) and below right Wim Rijsbergen who was unknown before the 1974 World Cup.

ROBBIE RENSENBRINK (RSC Anderlecht and Holland) Had Rensenbrink not pulled a thigh muscle and thus been only half fit for the World Cup Final, perhaps Holland would have won it. Certainly their effectiveness, in the image of his own, was greatly diminished. A left winger of pace, excellent control and bite, Rensenbrink made his name with DWS Amsterdam, and from there moved to Anderlecht; for whom his goals were invaluable in the 1974-75 European Cup. All in all, however, he played better for Holland that season than for Anderlecht; which led to speculations that he might be happier following the trail of another Anderlecht Dutchman, Jan Mulder, back to Holland. Born July 3, 1947.

WIM RIJSBERGEN (Feyenoord and Holland) A few weeks before the World Cup, there seemed little chance that the then 22 year old Wim Rijsbergen would be in the Dutch team. But injury to Barrie Hulshoff, the Ajax stopper, gave him his chance, and he played exceptionally well for them at centre-half. Blond and athletic, his chief disappointment was that a harsh tackle by Muller should injure him and cause him to leave the field in the Final itself. It was, in fact, his second Final within a few months, for he had also played a large part in Feyenoord's win over Tottenham Hotspur, in the UEFA Cup. Indeed, he scored his club's first goal in Rotterdam when they beat Spurs in the second leg. Born January 18, 1952.

ROLAND SANDBERG (Kaiserslautern and Sweden) A striking inside-forward famous for his partnership with Ralf Edström. They built it when playing for Atvidaberg in the Swedish Championship. When Atvidaberg won it in 1973, each scored 16 goals, Sandberg darting and probing to exploit the flicks and touches of the tall, slender Edström. In the World Cup, they were just as effective together, and Sandberg's goal against West Germany in Dusseldorf was a notable one. In 1973 he joined Kaiserslautern in the West German Bundesliga; their best attacker since the days of the Walter brothers, twenty years before. Born December 16, 1946.

Jurgen Sparwasser—facing page.

Roland Sandberg (above).

JURGEN SPARWASSER (1st, FC Magdeburg and East Germany) This dark haired, strongly built striker scored perhaps the most spectacular goal of the 1974 World Cup when, with a splendidly powerful burst down the right flank in Hamburg, he beat Maier, to give the West Germans their only defeat of the competition. The previous month, he had been a star of the Magdeburg team which defeated AC Milan in Brussels to win the European Cupwinners' Cup. A player with notable initiative and acceleration. Born June 4, 1948; winner of a Championship medal with Magdeburg in 1974.

JOSE MARIA ZE MARIA (Corinthians and Brazil) A perfect and greatly reminiscent successor to Djalma Santos; like himself, a strongly built, black, attacking right-back. Ze Maria had a very good 1974 World Cup; notable especially for the fine run and cross which brought a goal against Argentina. Born at Botucatu on May 18, 1949, he took his chance when Carlos Alberto dropped out of the international side, playing in the Independence Cup tournament of 1972, and keeping his place thereafter.

FOOTBALL SWORD
OF HONOUR 1975

PAUL BREITNER

THE 1972 GERMAN TEAM WAS THE BEST I PLAYED IN

says

PAUL BREITNER

of
Real Madrid

Even in the World Cup Final Breitner finds time and space to move up and attack . . . with Johan Cruyff dropping back to chase him.

SINCE I came to play for Real Madrid I have realised that football in Spain is quite a different thing from the game I knew in Germany. Here the players are just as eager to win and there is no great difference in sportsmanship, but now I realise that in Germany, football was a big business.

Here in Spain, football is more important than business or even politics. To the Spaniards, football is a way of life–so important that most other things are forgotten. In Spain, football is a passion, the most important things are bread and football.

I'm sure this is true throughout the country–and to the majority of Spaniards, but perhaps I feel it more because I am playing for Real Madrid. Whatever Real Madrid's form, they are always the team everyone wants to beat.

With Real Madrid on top of the league almost from the start of the season, every game has an

atmosphere all its own. Every game, no matter who we are playing, is like a Cup Final.

There is no great secret about Real Madrid's success. It revolves around hard work and the personality of our coach, Mr. Miljan Miljanic. We have not stopped working since the day we started pre-season training. Every day we work harder than the day before.

Paul Breitner (above) in possession and left, Yugoslav coach Miljan Miljanic who brought new methods and a new atmosphere to Real Madrid.

Our way of training seems to be completely new for Spain. We have many ways of training, mostly in small groups of three or four players, and the training is very, very hard.

Our coach is not only a fine trainer but also a very good man, and that I think is his greatest quality. A coach can only be good and have a good team if he is a good man, a good person. This is the secret of Miljanic's success and he has won the confidence of all the Real Madrid players.

Another reason behind Real Madrid's success is that we have good attacking players and we set out to play attacking football. Of course we have to adapt our tactics if we are playing away, say in Barcelona, but we don't ever play defensively in the real sense of the word.

I have been very lucky in my career as a footballer to have played for two very fine coaches, Udo Lattek being the coach of Bayern München when I was with them. To me, Udo Lattek was much more than a coach. I've known him for about nine years and for me, as well as for many other players he was like a brother . . . and a very fine friend.

Lattek had much in common with Miljanic in this respect. They both have qualities that are vital if a coach is to be successful–human understanding and warmth.

It is a tragedy that Bayern München are having a bad season and that Udo Lattek has gone. Their poor performances have nothing to do with my leaving. Their problems lie in the realm of the relationships between the player and the club. Clearly it is not a happy club at the moment.

I was very fortunate to join Bayern just at the right time. As an 18 year old I had much to learn and I learned a great deal about the game from Gerd Muller. Playing in the first team could have been an ordeal but with players with the skills of Beckenbauer and Muller around you, it makes everything easy.

It has been said that political differences created problems between myself and Franz Beckenbauer

Breitner wins the ball and carries it upfield before making a well judged pass.

51

and also the Bayern President, Wilhelm Neudecker. This is not true however, though we did disagree about certain things.

In my early days with Bayern we talked occasionally about politics. But I could see that the differences between us were so wide that it was useless to continue. But because Franz Beckenbauer and I had widely different political opinions, this did not mean that we could not play together.

My political thinking has not yet hardened. After all I'm still only 23 now. I cannot say that I am

Making his debut for Bayern München as an 18 year old, Breitner found that players like Gerd Müller (left) and Franz Beckenbauer (above) made it easy for him.

of the right, the left or the centre. All I have done is try to think for myself and create a way of thinking about politics. The process has only just started and I think I'll need another 15 or 20 years before I form a hard opinion. Perhaps when I am forty I will have settled for one particular line.

Neither is it true that I have given large sums of money to charity. I have said clearly and repeatedly in the past, that when I have finished playing I would like to complete my studies at University. Then I would like to create a school for handicapped children. But all that is the way of life that I hope to create for myself when I have finished playing football.

I signed a three year contract with Real Madrid that will expire in June, 1977. After that I would like to stay on with Real for another three or four years if I remain free from injury and all goes well. I have made up my mind to stay with Real Madrid for seven years–if they'll have me–because I like the club so much.

Combining attacking football with good results has often been a problem in football, but the West German team I played in around 1972 proved to me that it can be done. One of my greatest memories is the 3–1 victory when Germany beat England at Wembley. That's an example of attacking football at its best.

That 1972 team was the best I have played in– better than the side that won the World Cup last year. The European championship winning team of 1972 was a team of eleven stars, all fine players in their respective positions that blended together perfectly.

The 1974 team also fitted together neatly. But I think we won the World Cup because of effort–real work horses rather than a team of great skill.

I have never understood why Gunter Netzer couldn't find a place in the 1974 team. For me, Gunter Netzer was, and still is, one of the greatest players in the game. Only the German coach can explain why Netzer didn't get in the team.

My great philosophy for life is . . . 'live and let live'. Every man has to work out his own problems and make his own life . . . and there should be no interference. I must make my own life and I am not the kind just to live for ten or fifteen years as a footballer.

I have plenty of time to think, spending so much time travelling. So many planes, so many airports, spending several months each year in other countries. But I've settled down now to live for the present.

That, in my case means Real Madrid . . . from a player's point of view it must be the greatest club. I can't imagine any finer achievement in football than to play for Real Madrid.

It is so difficult for any other club to reach Real's standards. Here you are not just a footballer, but a man whose problems are always considered by people who are willing to help.

It's far more than just the money. It's the atmosphere–and feeling that you are part of a very warm organisation.

Rivelino (dark shirt) of Brazil shoots against Argentina.

SKILFUL, INTELLIGEN

a tribute to

PAUL BREITNER

★　　★　　★

AT ITS highest level, modern football is based on having real ability at the back and if the Ajax Amsterdam pair, Suurbier and Kro were the first into this field, Paul Breitner is probably the only modern full back to match them.

The Dutch pair showed all their skills in the 1974 World Cup, going forward to produce telling, final passes that in earlier generations had come only from orthodox wingers, but Breitner's abilities include the inclination and the ability, to go one step further and produce goalscoring shots.

Johnny Rep (left) the Ajax star that Breitner 'locked up' in the World Cup Final and (right), Breitner calmly scored from a penalty that levelled the score in that match.

FAST AND ATHLETIC

by I.F.B. Editor

Eric Batty

If he hasn't yet equalled the record of the Italian left back, Giacinto Facchetti, who scored more than 50 league goals, this is only because Breitner has been playing for such a relatively short time.

Though not a big man, Breitner gives nothing away in the air and being on the short side for a defender he has better balance and agility that are inevitably denied to bigger men. This balance enables him to recover more quickly against a skilful, feinting opponent so that he is rarely beaten on the ground.

The full backs who first distinguished themselves as skilful attacking players, Ajax Amsterdam and Holland stars Ruud Krol (on the left) and above, Wim Suurbier.

But as a full back, Breitner's defensive capabilities depend more on positional play and anticipation. These two qualities enable him to prevent many potentially dangerous situations from arising and also, perhaps equally important, take him into space to receive a pass from defensive colleagues under pressure.

In purely defensive terms it would be difficult to find a better or more reliable defender, but it is going forward that Breitner really stands out. In possession, he has all the confidence to hold the ball, all the composure to take opponents on, and the subtle instinct that tells him when to release the through pass that was once the preserve of the old fashioned inside forwards.

Photo right is Giacinto Facchetti of Inter-Milan and Italy who has scored more than 50 league goals. Below, part of the line up before the 1974 World Cup Final in Munich, scene of Breitner's greatest triumph yet.

Following his unexpected transfer to Real Madrid after the 1974 World Cup, his new club's Yugoslav manager Miljan Miljanic converted him into a midfield player, lining up alongside his countryman Gunter Netzer, to provide a solid base in the middle line that was the springboard for all their successes.

Other outstandingly gifted defenders who look good going forward only look composed because everything is going on in front of them. The test of all-round ability is to play further forward all the time, where so much goes on behind the player's

On the left, West German left winger Bernd Holzenbein with whom Breitner combined to earn a World Cup Final penalty kick. Below, another West German star in action, Jurgen Grabowski who played on the right wing.

back. Lining up at inside right, Breitner's positional sense remains just as keen as it was when everything was happening in front of him like an open book, simply there to be read. In addition, his physical qualities, speed in recovery after being beaten or by-passed, and pure stamina, enable him to play a more complete part in the team game than he did at full back.

Breitner first came into the headlines when he played in the memorable match at Wembley in April, 1972 in which West Germany beat England 3–1. Only 20 years old, with but three international appearances behind him, Breitner was inevitably overshadowed by his better known colleagues Franz Beckenbauer, Gunter Netzer and Gerd Muller. But he showed enough ability and composure under pressure to underline that he had star quality.

This was his real breakthrough into the big-time and in little more than two years he gained 26 caps and took every honour open to him.

That Wembley win was the German's biggest hurdle in their pursuit of the 1972 European Nations Cup and a few weeks later in Belgium, the Germans cantered to a triumph that even overshadowed the all-round skills of Ajax. It was also the high-point of the modern European game, the standard by which all other teams in the international arena will be measured for years to come.

Two years later, Breitner added a World Cup winners medal to his trophies and was one of the few German stars to live up to his reputation in 1974. In a German defence that was predominantly defensive, Breitner alone showed all his established

ability to go forward, scoring the only goal in the 1–0 win against Chile–with a real bomb of a shot from twenty yards. He scored again in the second stage, the first in a 2–0 win over Yugoslavia and had a superb game in the final. In the second half, with Holland pressing for a second goal, it was Breitner who headed out from under the German bar with Maier beaten following a Dutch corner.

With Johnny Rep of Ajax his immediate opponent, Breitner kept his winger locked up and still found time and space to go forward. With the Germans rocked by an early goal against them, only Breitner came forward regularly from the back four and it was he who created the opening for the equalising goal.

Winning possession by interception, Breitner moved upfield, covering 50 yards and exchanging a one-two before releasing a pass that sent left winger

Below, Breitner's former Bayern club-mate, Georg Schwarzenbeck.

Bernd Holzenbein away. The Dutch defence was torn apart and Wim Jansen, trying to cover, could only bring down Holzenbein for a clear penalty.

Both Muller and Beckenbauer, vastly more experienced, have been regular penalty takers and in the World Cup, Uli Hoeness successfully converted one. But in the final, with so much at stake it was Breitner who had been nominated. He calmly placed the ball on the spot, stepped back and then firmly planted the ball in the net, low to Jongbloed's right hand.

This was the peak of Breitner's career to date. In four years he had stepped out of the shadows of amateur football and at 22 was generally regarded as the best left back in the world.

It was only in the summer of 1970 that Breitner left the amateur club ESV Freilassing where he was coached by his father, persuaded to Bayern Munchen by their coach, Udo Lattek. Within a few months he had earned a regular first team place and at the end of his first season helped win the German FA Cup, beating 1st FC Koln in the final.

In the next three seasons between 1971–72 and 1973–74, Bayern took a hat trick of Bundesliga championship titles, finally winning the European Cup after a replay in the final with Atletico Madrid.

On top of his achievements with the West German national team, Breitner's Cup was full . . . and he was still only 23.

His transfer to Real Madrid for around £420,000 opened up new fields to conquer, new challenges and the switch to a midfield role. Breitner took it all in his stride and unlike Gunter Netzer and Johan Neeskens with CF Barcelona, settled immediately in the tougher Spanish game.

His new manager Miljan Miljanic said of him recently 'Breitner has fundamental virtues. He has a passion for the ball and the game, works harder and longer in training than his colleagues, is solid as a rock and is rarely injured. Above all he is a gentleman, and on the field is an example to all for his sportsmanship'.

Off the field, Breitner lives quietly with his wife Hildegard, and two little girls, one of them an adopted orphan from war-torn Vietnam.

For his considerable contribution to world football and his attitude to life as a human being, it would be difficult to find a more suitable recipient for International Football Book's Sword of Honour.

MACDONALD AND AYALA ARE THE TWO BEST MEN I HAVE FACED

BY
DAVE WATSON
THE SUNDERLAND AND ENGLAND STOPPER

NEWCASTLE'S Malcolm Macdonald is the centre forward I have the greatest respect for in English football. Peter Osgood is good too, though he seems to lack concentration and Duncan McKenzie is another you have to watch all the time but overall I think Macdonald is the top striker I've seen.

Osgood can be brilliant but he's patchy, often outstanding for ten minutes but then right out of the game for the next quarter of an hour. McKenzie's greatest asset is his totally unorthodox approach—you just never know what he's going to do next. But with Macdonald you have to be on your toes all the time and if there aren't too many trimmings in his game, you know that if you let him get by you, you'll never catch him—he's too quick.

Amongst the foreign teams I've played against for England the Yugoslavs were the side that impressed me most. They were strong and skilful too

Photo right is Dave Watson.

when we drew with them in Belgrade, and they didn't give the ball away often.

Fortunately though, the Yugoslav centre forward Ivan Surjak–a big fellow with plenty of real skill didn't bother me too much–largely because he dropped deep into midfield looking for the ball. He had a very elegant left foot and was very good on the ball but he didn't play upfield and perhaps he isn't really a natural centre forward.

Ruben Ayala, the Argentinian was a different matter, a real handful. He was quick too and saw things very early. If I was going to tackle he'd lay the ball off first time, but if he had time to turn on the ball and come at me, he did it very well.

Obviously the players who give you most trouble are those with a combination of Surjak's skill and Macdonald's speed–good enough on the ball to get by you and too fast to be caught once they're away. Happily though, that particular

combination doesn't often develop in one player.

Obviously I was delighted to be chosen to play for England but it can be very difficult. Nerves are one thing and frustration is another but though I naturally hope to keep my place you are constantly aware that if you play one bad game, you could be out.

This was particularly true of my first match for England, and the thought is never far away in the back of your mind. Playing at Wembley for Sunderland in the 1973 FA Cup Final was a totally different

You have to watch Malcolm Macdonald (below) heading a goal for England against West Germany, because he is so quick. 'Peter Osgood (photo right) now with South-ampton, is good too, but he is patchy,' says Dave Watson.

Sunderland have a better balanced attack now than we did with two natural wingers Denis Tueart (left) and Billy Hughes (below), says Dave Watson in action (below left) for England against Czechoslovakia. Photo right is Vic Halom, the Sunderland centre forward.

matter. First I think because I was with players that were familiar to me and also because we were inevitably the underdogs when we played Leeds United.

I know how it can be, for even with Sunderland when we meet a team from a lower division in a Cup tie you just can't get it out of your mind that 'they' are only a Third Division side or whatever. This psychological thing probably accounts for many of the shock wins by lesser teams in Cup ties.

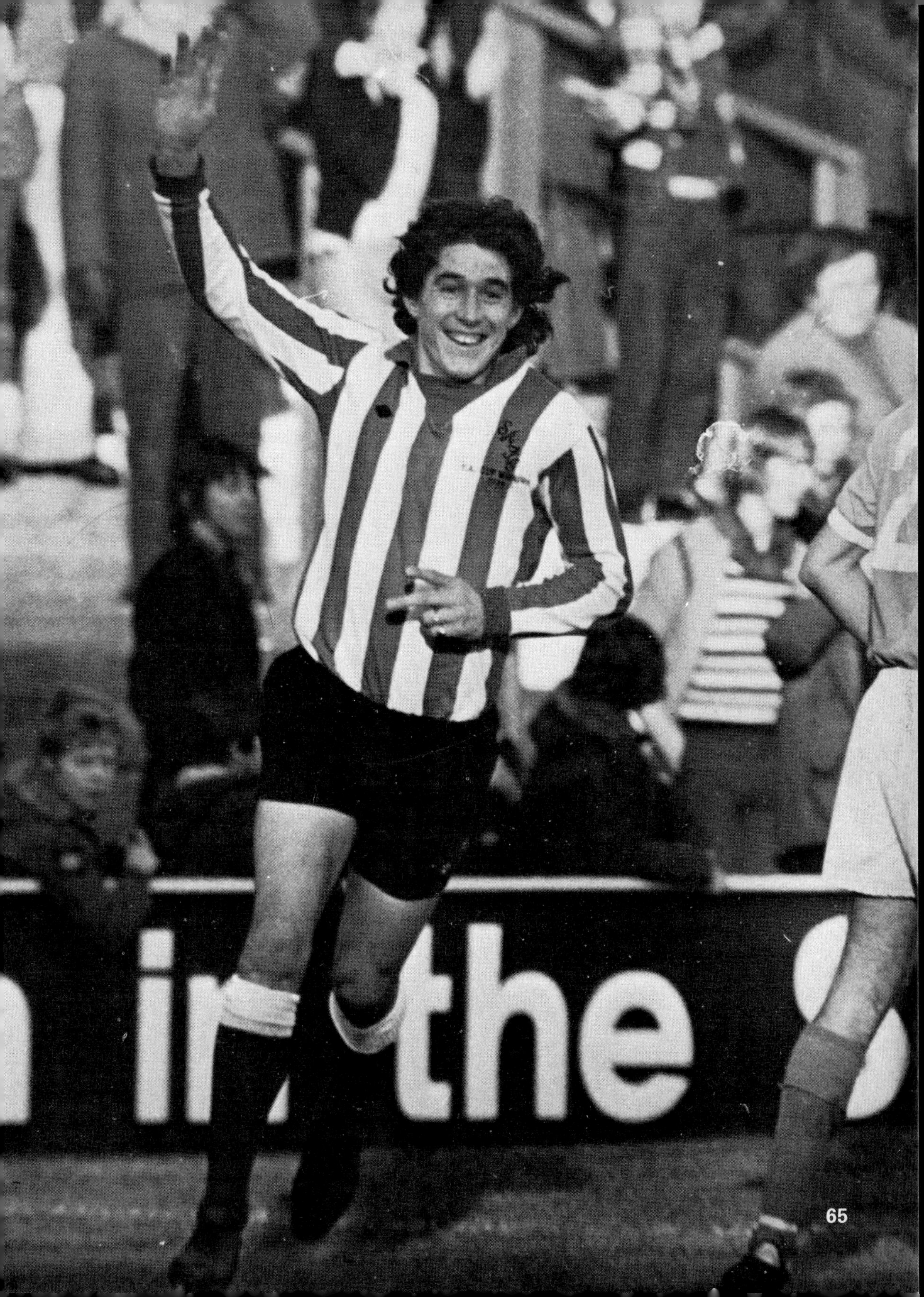
the

But I don't think this was the case when we beat Leeds, though it may have contributed to it. As I saw it, and I felt it out on the pitch at Wembley, we really threw Leeds out of their stride by attacking them every time we won possession of the ball.

After the first twenty minutes I could feel that we had Leeds worried. All our players were aggressive and very determined and the longer the game went on the more confident I became that we were going to win.

Looking back I don't think our success has been such a surprise. We had a lot of good players here at Sunderland and when our Manager Bob Stokoe arrived he re-organised the side and motivated the players. This ability to motivate the players is our boss's greatest asset–this and his knack of making shrewd moves in the transfer market.

Tony Towers who joined us from Manchester City proved a great buy last season and getting 'Pop' Robson from West Ham gave us a better balanced attack than we had before. It's difficult to compare our Cup winning team with the present

Ruben Ayala (below left) was a real handful at Wembley says Dave Watson. Tony Towers (above) has proved to be a great buy and (photo right) English referee Jack Taylor gives Germany's Wolfgang Overath a talking to.

side but I think the team of last season was better on balance.

With two natural wingers, Billy Hughes and Denis Tueart we never seemed as effective as we are now. Robson and centre forward Vic Halom have struck up a very good understanding and Robson has got a lot of his goals by knocking the ball to Halom and scoring off the flicks and touches he gets back. Robson is one of those players who is really goal-hungry, he needs to be scoring goals to be happy.

Though critics may complain that football isn't as entertaining as it used to be, it is certainly more professional these days. Almost every side in the top two divisions is really well organised and away from home–apart from Sunderland–it seems that most teams have copied the defensive tactics developed abroad. Away from home, most managers seem happy to settle for one point. Most that is, but not us, we want two points every time we play.

At international level it can be really frustrating playing against defensive sides, particularly at Wembley. The Czechs for example were willing to attack when they got the ball, though they weren't slow to scuttle back into defence when they lost it. But Portugal were quite different, setting out to get a draw at Wembley, right from the first minute.

The Portuguese only got down our end five or six times in the entire game and in these sort of circumstances you have to concentrate all the time. It is very easy, standing back from all the action to become isolated from the game and just become a spectator. That of course can be really dangerous and you have to be aware of it all the time. Certainly it's frustrating, but I don't know what the answer is if visiting teams really don't want to play.

Although I've earned comparatively few caps I'm already a veteran in the sense that I've played for England under three different managers, Sir Alf Ramsey, Joe Mercer and Don Revie. They all have one thing in common—their utter dedication to the game and their professionalism—but their approach is slightly different.

Sir Alf never left anything to chance, anticipating everything right down to the last detail. Meticulously professional in everything he did, I would say.

Joe Mercer was quite different, though of course everyone knew that he was only acting as a caretaker manager and never had a chance to have a look at the foreign teams we met during his brief period in charge. His attitude can fairly be summed up by words he used often . . . 'let them worry about us' and of course he believed in free expression by the players.

The emphasis with Don Revie appears to be to build confidence within the team and try to get that something extra from everyone. He keeps hammering away at the same theme—that the English players are the most professional in the world and that with only a little more we could be the best in the world.

I hope he's right and I'd love to help prove it in 1978.

AJAX IS NOT AJAX ANYMORE

By

BARRY HULSHOFF

THE STAR WHO MISSED THE WORLD CUP THROUGH INJURY

* * *

I believe Ajax is in trouble now because the players are being forced to play to a bad system. The manager, Hans Kraay, is developing new tactics based on hard workers. This was the reason why he had difficulties last season with an outstanding player like Piet Keizer who has now retired as a consequence.

Arie Haan, a very good midfield player is forced to play as a libero behind the defence, while the old sweeper, Horst Blankenberg is in midfield. I don't see the sense of that and I don't like it.

A similar thing has happened with Jan Mulder who is a natural centre forward, but he is being played in midfield too.

Barry Hulshoff (photo right) scored a vital goal against Norway to enable Holland to qualify for the World Cup but missed the finals through injury. On the left is Jan Jongbloed, the 'keeper who rose to stardom at 33.

These things have all created problems and should be much better arranged. But it is not my business and being out of the game with my injury for most of last season, I lost interest.

Sometimes I go to watch Ajax play, but I would much rather play with my two children or listen to modern music. It is strange, but my heart is dead for football, though I'm sure it would be different if I could play.

Of course Ajax lost a great deal when Johan Cruyff was transferred to CF Barcelona. In my opinion the team lost 30% of its brilliance and effectiveness. But perhaps even more important, the players who won the European Cup three times lost their ambition and the inspiration to work for new gold medals.

If Cruyff had stayed with Ajax I feel sure there would still have been this lack of ambition and the team would have been confronted with the same difficulties. But let me make it clear—there was no way to stop Cruyff going.

It was impossible to keep Cruyff in Holland,

Above, Rinus Michels, the coach who created the outstanding Ajax team and returned from Barcelona to lead Holland in the World Cup. Left, Johan Cruyff, the former Ajax super-star of whom Hulshoff (photo right) says 'there was no way to keep Cruyff with Ajax'.

because he was determined to go. He was offered too much money to be willing to stay with Ajax.

After he left, the problem for Ajax was to develop a new style of play that would keep them at the top of the international game. But as I have said, players like Wim Suurbier, Ruud Krol and Horst Blankenburg have lost the inspiration to fight.

Changing the club manager hasn't helped of course and we miss Rinus Michels very badly. He was the first coach to create a real professional team in Holland. He was a marvellous organiser, building up the team from nothing. He made real professionals out of amateurs. Without doubt, Michels led Ajax from obscurity to the very peak of European football.

71

He was a man who liked perfection. In training, during matches and in tactical ideas we did everything Michels wanted . . . and we got the results. Michels brought to the club players like Bals, Muhren, the Yugoslav Velibor Vasovic and Johan Neeskens. He coached them and taught players like Suurbier, Krol and myself how to play. Without him I would not have become the player I was.

Of course we won the European Cup for the third time after Michels left. But Stefan Kovacs, who took over from him was lucky that Michels had worked with Ajax before him, and that the players knew how to play in the shadow of Cruyff.

There were problems under Mr. Kovacs because he was only an artist. He didn't do anything on the training ground and was bad in tactics. Neither did he seem interested in the physical condition of the players. The only thing he was good at, was what I call the mental training of the players.

Before matches Kovacs talked with all the players and he certainly had the ability to inspire them. He knew all the details about other teams and

A lot of problems have been created within the Ajax team by playing players out of position, says Hulshoff. Arie Haan (above) has been playing sweeper and sweeper Horst Blankenberg (left) has been in midfield. Photo right, Barry Hulshoff (dark shirt) beats Belgium's Paul Van Himst in the air.

players in Europe and he could tell jokes like nobody else.

But he wasn't a good manager for Ajax in my opinion. Amongst other things he didn't seem to give enough attention to the younger players and I think that to be very important. Kovacs was very intelligent and perfect for public relations but he forgot about discipline and that came out and created problems after he had gone to France.

I am sure that there are many good young players in Holland who should get a chance with the big clubs like Ajax, PSV and Feyenoord. But Dutch officials have often preferred to spend a lot of money to bring in stars from foreign clubs. This is typically Dutch thinking–that foreign things will be better. I prefer the system in England, instead of spending money on foreign players we should keep the money within our own competition.

Ajax bought Rene Notten from FC Twente and that was a good deal in my opinion. But it was unwise to sign the former Hungarian star, Zoltan Varga and the German, Arno Steffenhagen.

I am convinced that Ajax can find the right kind of players in Holland, players with all the necessary qualities to become internationals. The scouting system at Ajax could be improved a great deal, but even so we have some very good youngsters. Players like Kraal, a defender, Alberts (midfield) and Kok, a forward, all have the possibility to reach the first team.

While I have been out injured, Johnny Dusbaba has taken my place and at 18 he was already one of the best in Holland. He is fast, has good skill and is brave and strong in the tackle. He needs to improve a bit in the air, but with encouragement from the club leaders ... and good players around him, he could become one of the best players in Europe.

My own future is very much in doubt. My troubles began during a game against NAC in Breda, in February, 1974. Sprinting to the ball, I suddenly turned my right knee. At first the doctors weren't sure what the trouble was.

I was out for three months and then played again in May, against PSV Eindhoven in a cup game. It was a disaster. I was in a lot of pain, couldn't sprint and had to play very carefully. Another month went by and finally it was decided that I should have an operation.

In a hospital in Amsterdam they took out the inside cartilage in my right knee. After that I started training again, but I never felt that the operation had been a success.

Two months into the 1974–75 season I made my come-back with Ajax, playing in a league game against Roda JC in the south of Holland. The

manager told me to play for only 40 minutes to avoid too much strain, but everyone thought I would quickly regain my form of a year before.

Then in November we had an important game away to Feyenoord in Rotterdam. No one in the club seemed to think they had a chance to win without me. It seemed that my presence would be a good psychological influence on the team. I played in midfield but it was terrible. I was much too slow, but also I was really afraid to play all out, and we lost 2–1.

Still they tried to get me back into the team. Manager Hans Kraay told me I should fight for my place–but I realised that was just a bad joke.

At the end of November I was back in the team again away to PSV, another difficult game. I was given the task of eliminating Ralf Edström, the magnificent heading specialist. We drew, but again I didn't feel right and in the days following the game my knee was very painful.

I had one more game before the end of the year against FC Den Haag but only played 45 minutes. After that I decided to stop playing for a long rest. I asked the club to seek the opinions of two neutral doctors and they agreed. One of the specialists recommended a new operation, the other advised me to do special training without the ball.

The second suggestion was the most attractive to me because the muscles in my leg were not strong enough. Jan Mulder had a similar problem in 1974 and he recovered as a result of physical training. Therefore I did the things he did in training . . . without the ball.

Everywhere I went unless it was too far, I rode a bicycle and two or three days a week I was busy rowing. Then I began lifting weights. If everything goes well I hope to start in full training again for the 1975–76 season, but I realise that my playing days might well be over.

Assuming that I make a complete recovery I will stay with Ajax until my contract expires in June, 1976. I cannot say right now whether I will sign again for Ajax, but obviously, with my fitness in doubt, none of the other big clubs in Holland would take the risk of offering me a contract.

If I am lucky, I would like to go on playing for another three or four years. After that I would like to be a coach–not a manager. I enjoy talking with young players and would like to coach, experiment

The best Ajax player now, Gerrie Mühren.

with tactics, to organise things and work with a team that plays clean, sporting football.

Players like Cruyff and Keizer crop up only once in 25 years. They weren't the products of any special circumstances, they just appeared. Unfortunately we don't have such players any more in Holland.

The best player now is Gerrie Mühren who plays in midfield for Ajax. He can do everything with the ball, even more than Keizer in his time. Wim Van Hanegem is still a great midfield player too, but we have no really superb attacking players now and it will be difficult for Holland to make a come-back.

I think the managers should give the players more freedom to play their own game. Dutch football is going the way of England.

There is no place now for individual ability. The players have to do their job–just as the manager tells them.

In these circumstances there is little chance that we shall see a new Keizer or a new Cruyff.

THE GAME MUST SELL ITSELF BETTER

By

DENIS TUEART

of

Manchester City

THE football industry is in a state of decline and the fact that attendances are dropping at professional level is only the tip of the iceberg. What is not so obvious–because no serious study has yet been undertaken–is the plain fact that more and more youngsters are drifting away from football, both as spectators and players.

The complete problem can be viewed at three separate points; falling attendances at professional level; the almost total disappearance of 'street football' and the growing participation in other sports.

Attendances at the professional game will always fluctuate because in every Division of the Football League, success generates new enthusiasm. But every season, success, in terms of being top of their league is restricted to a mere handful of clubs. The other clubs are being hit more and more.

Older generations recognised long ago that there was a direct link between the standing of football and the numbers that played in back streets, back fields and school playgrounds. Even in my time,

and I'm still in my early twenties, I spent hours as a boy playing football in kick-about games. We used to play on, even after dark, with lamp posts providing the 'floodlighting'. But today it is rare that anyone sees youngsters kicking a ball about. They have other things to occupy their time.

I can myself testify to the growth in popularity of sports like squash and badminton that not long ago were fringe games played by only a handful of people. Squash I took up when I was with Sunderland but my association with badminton goes back to my schooldays. Since then, with my wife also enjoying badminton we began to play together . . . and still play regularly.

This growing participation in sport has not passed un-noticed. When I was at Sunderland I was taking a course in Commercial and Recreational Management at the Tees-Side Polytechnic, and

Colin Bell of Manchester City executes a perfect volley while on England duty.

time'. But in my opinion they prefer midfield because you can enjoy the game there without feeling the pressures and responsibilities that are carried by goalkeepers and goalscoring forwards. If you play up front to get goals or you play in goal to prevent goals being scored, you just cannot hide as you can in midfield.

The real problem that the game is facing today is internal pressure on coaches and managers. That pressure is passed on to the players and the result is that fear dominates almost everywhere. Fear of defeat, fear of relegation, fear of being knocked out of the Cup. Fear and pressure.

The youngsters feel this too. Even in school games they are under pressure to win. The result is that more and more youngsters are turning to other sports for their relaxation, games that they can play just for fun. Even those that play football feel the pressure and I've already indicated that the majority are seeking to avoid the biggest pressures by playing in midfield.

Willie Donachie (above) one of the most popular Manchester City players and (right) Rodney Marsh. 'I have to try and anticipate what they will do,' says Denis Tueart.

was told that the leisure activities are Britain's biggest growing industry. More and more people are taking part in sport today—other sports, not football—and though it's obviously good for the public as a whole it doesn't do football any good.

The game has only itself to blame, for in my opinion it has failed to sell itself to the public. At top level the back room boys, the managers and coaches, must make football more entertaining if they are to bring the crowds back. At a lower level, coaches and schoolteachers have to sell the game to the youngsters so that they give up more of their leisure time to playing football.

At the lower level there is another problem too, in that most good young players today want to play in midfield. Most youngsters will tell you that they prefer midfield 'because they are involved all the

At every level, schoolteachers, coaches and managers must somehow put the pleasure back into the game. Let the kids enjoy playing football and take the pressure off the professionals too. Football has to be sold today–sold to everyone with the emphasis on enjoyment.

For myself I still enjoy playing but I know that many professionals don't like the pressures under which they have to play. The pressure is greater of course since I left Sunderland for Manchester City but there are compensating features.

I didn't really want to leave the North East where I still have many friends in Newcastle and Sunderland. After I'd helped Sunderland to win the FA Cup, half the Sunderland players attracted attention from First Division clubs.

According to the newspapers, Derby and Liverpool were interested in me but perhaps that was just paper-talk. Anyway, Manchester City came first and after talks with their officials I made up my mind to go. First Division football has to be the aim of every professional and though I didn't specially want to leave Sunderland, my ambition and the recognition that football is essentially a short career left me with little choice.

Once I had settled in Manchester, I found that the people there and in Cheshire, where I live, are very much like those in the North East. The big difference is in the atmosphere round the game. With so many big names in the Manchester area the newspaper and television coverage is much greater.

It took me around a month to settle in the First Division and then I began to realise that it is both

Mick Doyle of Manchester City in an aerial duel with Martin Busby (white hoops) of Queens Park Rangers.

easier and more difficult to play in the top class. In the First Division, opponents seem to allow you to play a bit more. Apparently, they have more respect for each other compared with the Second Division. There the skill level in most teams–with one or two exceptions–is not so high, and the players make up for this lower level of ability with harder work.

It's more difficult however, to play in a side like Manchester City with so many players of exceptional ability. Colin Bell, Joe Royle, Rodney Marsh, Asa Hartford, Willie Donachie and Mike Summerbee are all gifted and experienced players. They respect individual ability, just as the club does, but surrounded by so many good players it's more difficult to fit in.

With so many of my team mates having a high degree of individual ability, they are more likely to try to do out of the ordinary things. I have to read situations and try to anticipate what my colleagues are going to do and that's far more difficult than in the Second Division.

I was 24 when I first played for Manchester City and I soon realised what I'd missed and wished I could have started off in the top flight. Looking back, born in Newcastle and a great United fan, I watched them all the time, played myself whenever I could and in the school holidays I was up at the Newcastle training ground, collecting autographs. But it was a Sunderland scout, Charlie Ferguson who took me to his club and I've never regretted that decision to join them.

With City, the pressure was on all last season, playing like real champions at Maine Road but finding it difficult to be successful in away games. Away from home, most teams are more defensive and our natural game is to attack. We go at them at home, looking for goals and have few real problems. But away from home I found that other teams were more willing to push players forward and because we still tried to play attacking football, we became stretched at times and exposed our goal.

Through trying to play real old fashioned, attacking football, we found ourselves at a disadvantage. Why teams should play defensively when they visit us at Maine Road is simply explained . . . we are back to fear again.

No matter what kind of work you do, there has to be job satisfaction and though I get it and thoroughly enjoy my football, I know that the vast majority of professionals do not. Somehow the back-room boys have to reduce the pressure on the players generally and sell the game to the public. In my opinion, if the players enjoy taking part in a game, then the public will enjoy it too and the fans will come pouring back everywhere.

Flashback to Tueart's Sunderland days with whom he won an F.A. Cup Winners medal and learned that leisure activities are the fastest growing industries in Britain. Football however is declining while other games catch on.

FRANCISCO

MARINHO

of Botafogo

◆ ◆ ◆

BRAZIL'S 1974 World Cup, though they took third place, was a somewhat inglorious one. Their team played, by and large, without the customary flair and flow. But there were consolations, and none more so than that of the 22 year old left-back, Francisco Marinho of Botafogo.

To say that Marinho is a thoroughly modern, attacking full-back would be correct but insufficient. He is very much in the direct tradition of Brazilian 'volantes', reminding us that though Brazil adopted the third back game in the early 1950's, gave the world 4-2-4 in 1958, and 4-3-3 in 1962, they have always tended to think of full-backs in the fashion of the old wing-halves; flank players whose task it was to go forward as well as to defend.

This Marinho does with spectacular success. He is tall, very strong and very fast; in full motion, he is a very hard man to stop. He has, moreover, a very powerful left foot.

It is no surprise to learn that soon after he had come to the famous Botafogo club of Rio, in 1972,

Francisco Marinho, Brazil's big discovery of the 1974 World Cup (on the left) and his namesake Mario Marinho, now with CF Barcelona, who played with him in West Germany (right).

he was being asked and allowed to take the free kicks, despite the presence in the team—as he himself remarked—of such established 'shots' as Jairzinho, Fischer, Omar and Brito.

Anyone who doubted the power of Marinho's free kicks must have had them set comprehensively at rest in Brazil's opening game of the World Cup, when a fulminating dead ball kick from outside the box provoked a notable save from Maric, in the Yugoslav goal.

For this attribute, Marinho, evidently a modest young man, pays tribute to the coach he had when he played for the Nautico club of Recife: Gradim. 'I am happy above all for Gradim,' he says. 'He saw at once that I had a strong shot and he began to train me to take dead ball kicks. His lessons have been profitable for me.' Indeed they have; Brazilian goalkeepers may feel that he has learned them only too well, for those free kicks are the terror of defences.

The Brazilian full-back he reminds me of is Nilton Santos, that splendid, swarthy figure who played in Brazil's World Cup teams of 1954, 1958 and 1962; when, at the age of 36, he won his second gold medal. There is, of course, no similarity between them in colouring or racial origin, Nilton cutting as characteristically Latin American a figure as Marinho a Nordic one. Since there are very few blonds to be found in that northern region where Marinho was born at Natal, it has been suggested that he is of Dutch origin, the Dutch traders having plied that part of the world in the 18th century. In fact, I believe his ancestors were Italian.

Botafogo brought him to Rio late in 1972. At first, says Marinho, the other players tended to laugh at his provincial ways, the questions he asked, but by and large adaptation was easy; though he could have asked for an easier debut than to play against Santos, at the Maracana Stadium.

'Imagine the nightmare,' says Marinho. 'I had never seen the Maracana, 200,000 capacity and the flags, chants and fireworks dancing above me and exploding in my head. I felt a little drunk. Then I brusquely remembered that Santos were lining up against me, and the great Pelé; the King whom I'd dreamed of knowing and playing against since childhood.'

Brazil World Cup boss Mario Zagalo (below). He knew how good Francisco Marinho was for he was manager of Botafogo too.

Free kicks were a feature of the 1974 World Cup as defences get tighter. Above left, Rivelino bangs one in against Argentina and (below left) Vladislav Bogicevic tries one for Yugoslavia against Sweden. Francisco Marinho is himself a hot shot with dead ball kicks.

'Good God, what a baptism of fire! But I strove to convince myself: "Either you establish yourself now or else you're going to make everyone smile and you'll have the career of a meteor." For some five minutes I was ill at ease, but after taking a deep breath I gained confidence when I played an easy ball, and I recovered all my aplomb. I'd done it.'

Indeed he had. When the Brazilian team made its European tour of 1973, Zagalo picked the then 21 year old full-back. He had no great expectations, as Marco Antonio, a year older than he and vastly more experienced, was also on the trip; indeed, he played only against Sweden. But by 1974, the roles had been reversed. There was no way of keeping the spectacular Marinho out of the World Cup side.

Marinho is a lively, cheerful, happy go lucky young man; qualities which led to an embarrassing situation when he returned from the 1973 tour. In Copenhagen, he had, in his ingenuousness, bought a blue film, which he proceeded to show for the first time at . . . a family reunion, which included his 16 year old fiancée from Bahia.

No permanent harm was done. The marriage duly took place.

During the World Cup, he was always the one to start the team singing in the coach. One remembers that on the only occasion one saw him commit a bad foul, in the third place match against Poland, he came back to shake the hand of his victim. 'He's a big kid,' the other Brazilians say of him, 'but this youthful spirit is so healthy, so natural, so spontaneous, so endearing that we cannot grudge him his little excesses and exaggerations.'

Francisco de Chaves Marinho, to give him his full name, no doubt owes to this exuberant temperament the speed of his ascent in first Brazilian, then in international football. In bygone years, one of the chief preoccupations of the Brazilian directors and coaches was to bridge the great gap between the first and the second, for players who often came from very primitive backgrounds. This was no doubt one of the reasons why Brazil flattered to deceive for so long, before finally carrying off the World Cup in 1958.

In Marinho they have a full-back who could equal or even beat Nilton Santos' record of three World Cups; for at his age, Nilton had yet to play a World Cup tournament. Indeed, when the 1950 World Cup was played in Brazil itself, he was a 24 year old reserve.

Whether Marinho will emulate Nilton by winning two World Cup medals is another matter. Between now and 1978, Brazil will have to find a few forwards and midfield players of the same, exceptional category as himself. Sad that he should be made the scapegoat of his club's poor form in 1974-75; sadder still that his wife should lose their first child. But Marinho is resilient enough to recover.

On the left (facing page) Pelé, the super-star of Brazilian football, signing autographs during the World Cup where he was a spectator. Francisco Marinho, in World Cup action on the right, played his first league game for Botafogo against Santos FC—marking Pelé, the idol of his boyhood.

I HATE TO WATCH FOOTBALL

By
DAVE THOMAS
Q.P.R. and England winger

Thomas (left) in action and, below, getting a wigging from a referee.

ALTHOUGH I enjoy my life as a professional footballer, both playing and training, one of the things I dislike most is watching other people play. When I was young, living up in the North East I used to go with my father to watch the amateur side West Auckland play regularly. In those days of course there were some good amateur sides in that area, including Bishop Auckland and Crook Town.

But somehow, I cannot explain exactly why, I just can't sit and watch other teams play now, whether it is a team we are going to meet in the near future or even the Reserves or Youth side of my own club. It isn't that I'm not interested, I just don't seem to be made for watching the game. I always feel frustrated watching others–wanting to get out there and play myself.

The only exception to this is watching football on television, which I do regularly. Then because of my home surroundings and the remoteness that is inevitable with television, I don't seem to have the itch to join in.

Dave Thomas left Burnley for Queens Park Rangers because he just couldn't get on with manager Jimmy Adamson (photo left). He doesn't score many goals himself which he recognises as some weakness in his make-up but says he gets enormous satisfaction from laying on chances for Rangers star strikers Don Givens (facing page) and (above) the tremendously gifted Stan Bowles.

89

I've travelled around in England a bit during my life, born at Kirkby-in-Ashfield, in Nottinghamshire, but when I was only a few weeks old my parents moved back to the North East. From there I went to Burnley and on to London. I live just outside London now and though there's no doubt there are more things to do in London if you want the gay life, I'm what you might call the relaxed type that rarely goes out. I spend most of my evenings at home with my family and my only real hobby is gardening.

In fact I never really wanted to come to the South of England but at Burnley I just didn't seem able to get on with the manager Jimmy Adamson. There wasn't any specific point on which we quarrelled–we just never seemed able to get along together for long. I suppose things happen like that in every walk of life. Looking back I would just say that I think the two of us had such different personalities.

I'll always be grateful to Burnley for giving me my chance. But in the end I was glad to get away, though at first it seemed as if I might have made a wrong move. For a start I didn't really want to move to the South and above all I really wanted a chance in First Division football. At the time I joined them, Rangers were in the Second Division, though we soon put that right and all in all things have worked out fine.

Even so, I think my heart will always be in the North East. That's where my parents are and my wife's family are all up there too.

When I got my first full cap–going on as a substitute against Czechoslovakia–I was the first real winger to play for England for some years. But I wasn't always a winger. I can remember playing left back as a schoolboy when I was about seven, but I've always been an attacking player.

Later I moved to left half and then I became an inside forward. Almost every youngster these days wants to be an inside forward because playing in midfield you are always involved in the game. That's where the action is.

Later I got a schoolboy cap for England as a left winger but at Burnley I was a midfield player and it was Rangers that converted me to the right wing.

I wouldn't like to say for sure whose idea it was to play me on the wing. I think what happened was that Gordon Jago, our manager, Bobby Campbell the coach and Terry Venables the captain, all put their heads together and the outcome was that they asked me to play on the wing.

Again it was one of those things that worked out fine for me and ultimately enabled me to play for

Dave Thomas in action (right) in Q.P.R.'s change colours. Photo left shows a human pyramid topped by Birmingham City's Joe Gallagher (dark shirt) and Gordon McQueen of Leeds United.

the full England team which was an ambition I'd long had. Though I hope naturally to get more caps, that first one completed my set for previously I had played for England at every other level.

There seems little doubt that I would have a better chance of earning a regular place for England if I scored goals. But somehow I just don't seem to have the knack and when I get a goal it's a day to hang the flags out. I've always admired Malcolm Macdonald for his attitude to goals, though I have heard other people criticising him for being selfish. He is one of those with a real longing to burst the net and I envy him this.

I don't think there's anything one can do to change your make-up in points like this. Really top quality goal scorers are born with this lust for goals . . . and I just don't have it.

In a strange way I'm sure I get just as much pleasure out of making goals for others as Macdonald does in scoring himself. Over the season I suppose I must lay on chances for something over twenty goals scored by my team-mates and that satisfies me. After all, football is a team game and the important thing is to get goals. Never mind whose name goes in the scorers list, as long as they keep coming.

Of course with Rangers we've got Stan Bowles and Don Givens who have the scoring knack, as well as a lot of other good players. I'm more than happy playing my part in helping to set up chances for them. If I am critical about myself, I suppose I am not selfish enough but that's the way I'm made.

We got off to a bad start in the league last season but I'm sure we will come again. Looking back I think I would agree with many critics who said we were playing the most attractive, attacking football in the top flight in the 1973-74 season. But at that time we were new to the big clubs, unknown quantities, and the individual abilities of our players were something of a surprise in the top flight. That made things a little easier for us, but it re-bounded the next season when we had become known, and helped create a few problems for us. Now it's more difficult for us to put our attacks together as we did, but in the middle of last season we all felt things were beginning to go better again and I'm very optimistic about the future.

Photo left shows Thomas' Q.P.R. clubmate Gerry Francis on England duty. On the right (upper photo) Don Givens scores against Derby County with Thomas looking on. Below right, Thomas appeals for a goal in the England–Portugal game but the ball miraculously rebounded after hitting the bar and a post and the referee said 'No'.

As I've already said I don't like watching and this applies to being substitute too. I'm not complaining about being asked to be the substitute; after all someone's got to do it and as a professional footballer it is part of the game and has to be accepted. But going onto the pitch cold, and not warmed up mentally either, presents problems that the average spectator probably doesn't appreciate.

The use of substitutes, except in the case of a serious injury is always a bit of a gamble that can go either way. Luckily for me, when I went on for England at Wembley I got into the game right away, which is the difficult bit, and things worked out fine. Now I hope there'll be more chances to show what I can do for England but please, when you're watching, don't barrack a player who comes on as a substitute and doesn't play too well. I know it isn't easy unless you happen to be lucky, as I was.

Clearly the game is changing and going to change even more in the future. I am personally divided on what seems likely to be one of the big issues coming to the fore, the question of freedom of contract. I can see the logic of it in principle and I know that the very top layer of players will benefit, but I'm more than a bit worried about the overall effect it will have on the game if it goes through.

In particular I feel sorry for the fellows playing for Third and Fourth Division clubs who can't be making much money. They are the ones that will suffer though perhaps they will be financially better off as part-time professionals with a job on the side outside football.

Some of them possibly like the idea of being a professional footballer, just for the local prestige but the only reason I can think of that keeps most of the lads playing for low wages in the Third and Fourth Divisions is the hope that they'll be picked up by a First Division club and get a crack at the top class. Clearly their chances of making the breakthrough will be more limited without the advantage of full time training.

Pre-match ceremony before the England–Portugal game at Wembley. England captain Emlyn Hughes exchanges gifts with Portuguese centre half Humberto Coelho who plays for Benfica.

Eric Batty writes about

GRZEGORZ LATO

of Poland

'THE BEST RIGHT WINGER IN THE WORLD'

★   ★   ★

A portrait of Grzegorz Lato taken during the World Cup in which he was the highest goal scorer in the competition with 7 goals. Lato plays for a comparatively unknown club, Stal Mielec.

TWENTY years ago, in the era of Stan Matthews and Tom Finney, wingers rarely played an active part in any game for more than a few minutes in total. On that basis alone, despite the damage that a player like Matthews could create, wingers had to adapt or die out, because in the modern game it is essentially an eleven-a-side, all action effort.

Work-rate is a term that has been abused, some suggesting that hard-working players were better than skilful ones when in reality everyone can agree that skilled, intelligent players who work hard, are what is required. Nevertheless, wingers who stood on the halfway line, waiting for a colleague to give them the ball were destined to disappear. They had to adapt and play a more complete role . . . or go.

At first, as exemplified by England in 1966, wingers were done away with. But since then a new breed of winger has developed, epitomised by Jairzinho who was a resounding success at outside right for Brazil when they won the World Cup in

1970. But quite the best of the new style wingers that I have seen is Poland's Grzegorz Lato.

Born in April, 1950, Lato developed as a goal-scoring centre forward with his relatively unknown club, Stal Mielec. But at that time, the hero of all Poland was centre forward Wlodzimierz Lubanski, an international since he was 16 and an automatic choice. Positively brilliant in every aspect of the game, Lubanski was king and to oust him would have been unthinkable. Thus it was that Lato's first two caps, back in 1971, were earned on the left wing.

At that time Lato was only 21 and he failed to make any real impact. Legia's Robert Gadocha

regained his place on the left wing, apparently leaving Lato in the wilderness.

Fortunately for him, Poland's national squad had been taken over in December, 1970 by a man who was destined to put Polish football on the international map at last, Kazimierz Gorski. Though Lato was omitted, there is no doubt that Gorski kept his eye on the Mielec striker.

In Poland's 1971-72 season, Lato hit 12 goals for Stal, a huge success for one so young, compared to Lubanski's 14 for the champions, Gornik Zabrze, which made him the top scorer in Division I. The following season, Lato went one better in two senses—scoring 13 goals and earning top place in the scorers list, but still not making the breakthrough to the national team.

Grzegorz Lato in action on the left and (above) Kazimierz Gorski, the Polish national team manager who converted him to be a right winger. On the opposite page, upper photo shows Brazil's Jairzinho in action, the forerunner of the new-style winger. Photo below shows Holland's Arie Haan in possession in the World Cup Final.

At the end of that season, Lato was still playing centre forward for Stal and when England were beaten 2–0 in Chorzow, Banas, Lubanski and Gadocha were Poland's front three. Even when Lubanski went off, injured in the second half, it was Lato's club-mate, Jan Domarski, who played on the left wing for Stal, who went on as substitute.

But by this time the stage was set for Lato's re-entry into the international arena. Preparing for the vital World Cup qualifying games in the autumn

Poland's midfield generals whose passes launched Lato in many assaults on goal and contributed much to the Poles' successes in the World Cup. Below is Henryk Kasperczak, Lato's clubmate at Mielec. On the right is the extremely gifted Kazimierz Deyna of Legia Warsaw.

of 1973, Gorski took Poland's squad off to the United States and Canada in August and it was on this tour that Gorski played a hunch and switched Lato to the right wing.

Back from North America, the Poles visited Bulgaria for a friendly match and it was there, in Varna, amongst 50,000 Bulgarians that I first saw Lato. Poland won 2–0 with Lato in magnificent form, a revelation on the right wing, getting both goals.

The thing that first struck me about Lato was his sheer pace. Against an 8 man defence the Bulgarians organised, the Polish midfield generals Deyna and Kasperczak hit a volley of superbly flighted long passes and Lato, playing a game that can only be described as a right winger-cum-centre forward, was the target for many of them.

Just before half time, a good bout of inter-passing by the Poles drew the Bulgarians tight on their men. Then came the sudden long pass that was headed on

Photo right shows Aston Villa goalkeeper Jim Cumbes carrying match-winner Ray Graydon after Villa's League Cup Final success over Norwich City at Wembley.

through the middle by Domarski . . . and there was Lato, away, and flying like an Olympic sprinter to score, right footed, with a hard low cross shot.

In the second half Lato exploded. With the Bulgarian defence caught square, a 50 yard pass flew over their entire defence and Lato was away again, cutting in from the right. Outstripping the entire defence he had only the 'keeper to beat and as Goranov advanced, Lato steadied himself and slipped the ball past the 'keeper at just the right moment.

The Poles might have got seven or eight goals that day. Lato, who had several other good shots and one superb diving header brilliantly saved, might have had four or five on his own. Lato had arrived. I knew it, and so too did Kazimierz Gorski.

At Wembley, when Poland qualified for the 1974 World Cup at England's expense Lato had a comparatively quiet game. The Poles were playing for a draw and only counter-attacking at intervals through Jan Domarski (who hit the vital goal) and Lato. But in the second half, Lato's relative inexperience cost him a superb chance of early glory. A fine pass from Kazimierz Deyna split the England defence and Lato, sprinting through the middle was away on his own with only goalkeeper Shilton to beat. Unfortunately for him, Lato was deceived by England players who stood appealing for offside. He hesitated, almost stopping, to look across at the linesman, half expecting to hear the whistle which never came. That moment of hesitation was enough to give Shilton his chance and Lato's glory goal had slipped away.

A few months later however, Lato covered himself with glory in the World Cup final stages where he scored seven goals to take the top scorers title as Poland, desperately unlucky in a critical game against West Germany took third place.

Fittingly, it was Lato who scored the decisive goal in the third place match against Brazil in the Munich Olympic Stadium. The match itself was a disappointment, as third place games so often are, but Lato's goal was brilliantly taken.

Receiving a ball at his feet, out wide on the right, Lato shuffled forward in the old Matthews-style against two Brazilian defenders who, with other Poles running square looking for a pass, were reluctant to commit themselves to a tackle. Lato

came on until, just outside the penalty area, h feinted to pass and took off, outside the back on hi own before cutting in and slipping the ball past th Brazilian goalkeeper into the far corner of the net.

Even Lato's greatest admirers would never equat him with Matthews–but he has a high degree c skill with the ball. Neither can he be compared wit Gerd Muller, 'der bomber' . . . at his best, and n Pole would accept that Lato was a better all-roun player than Lubanski. But what Lato has, is a bit c everything. He has pace, speed off the mark, fin anticipation of the moment to break in pursuit of defence-splitting through pass and he gets goals wit both head and foot.

In the World Cup, Lato got an individualisti goal against Brazil already described. He score with full blooded shots with his right foot and h headed a fine goal at the near post from a left win cross–after sprinting twenty yards to get there.

What Lato has can be summed up in a phrase. H is the modern winger *par excellence* and his greates asset is perhaps the fact that he is not a natura winger at all but a converted centre forward.

As such he is always looking for goals, roving al along the line of attack from right to left, and he ha the pace to outstrip most tight-marking opponents What makes him unique however, is that he appear able to play quite naturally as a centre forward o the right wing.

When the Poles are forced to defend, Lato drop deep–making himself easy to find with a pass. I he gets the ball he has the skill to go by his man an the intelligence to use the ball early by passing o crossing the ball to a well placed colleague. But i the Poles build their attack through the middle, h is always alert, ready like a sprinter on his blocks t dart forward in search of a pass that will take hi through to goal, cutting in from the right.

In a more orthodox approach, Lato can also beat men on the right and take on all comers for pace t get down the far end and cross the ball like a orthodox winger. But when the attack develops down Poland's left flank then Lato moves inside t become a second centre forward, ready, willing an as he proved in the World Cup, very much able t snap up half chances and turn them into goals.

Lato doesn't play ON THE RIGHT WING a his predecessors did–he plays *from* the right win and uses all his talents to the full.

Poland's talented Robert Gadocha, naturally right footed but played on the left to accommodate Lato. Gadocha now plays in France for Nantes FC.

PAUL MADELEY

of LEEDS UNITED a

'BEING ADAPTABLE IS A

'GLAND says

DVANTAGE'

'I am sure Don Revie will be
able to build a successful
England side'

WITH Leeds United I have played in a
variety of positions and particularly
when you are first starting in the game,
being adaptable is a great advantage. That's how it
was for me anyway and I think my adaptability has
been of value to my club too, for last season I spent
three months doing Norman Hunter's job while he
was out injured.

I joined Leeds United when I was seventeen,
after playing for a local club against Leeds Youth
team and presumably making an impression. I was
a centre half then, probably because I was bigger
than most boys of my age and turned professional
almost immediately. In those days the apprentice-
ship scheme was only just starting but I was too old
anyway.

*Paul Madeley (left) has played in many positions but
says 'at top level I am a right back.' Last season he stood in
for his Leeds United colleague Norman Hunter (right)
while he was out of action following a cartilage operation.*

I played a few games for Leeds back in their Second Division days and due to my knack of being able to do a useful job anywhere in defence I certainly got more first team games than I would otherwise. I wasn't an overnight success in the sense that I claimed a first team place at once, but with someone unfit to play almost every week I was able to keep a more or less regular place in the first team by standing in for one or other of the regulars. I'm

sure that switching around, particularly in thos early days enabled me to become a better all-roun player.

Whether I like switching around or bein switched about is probably the question I've bee asked most often, and during my career I'v changed my mind about it several times. I know many players would envy me, Norman Hunte amongst them, for I know he's just bursting to g forward and try to play creatively. I was quit happy doing his job in the back four and I'v probably reached the point where I don't min where I play, happy to settle in one position for while and just as happy if I'm switched again.

Getting into the England team is a different thing altogether, though I know Emlyn Hughes ha played full back on both sides and also in midfield

Two of Leeds United's key men, Johnny Giles (left) flicking the ball over an opponent's head and Billy Bremner (above). On the right, Don Revie, the manager during Leeds' successful years meets a new opponent, Czech manager Vaclav Jezek. Right (above) Duncan McKenzie bursts through the middle for Leeds against Wimbledon.

But being very honest I cannot see myself playing for England anywhere but at right back. It might still be an advantage being adaptable, in getting into the England squad and obviously the experience is invaluable, but at international level it is now so specialised and the problems are so varied that few players can really reach the required standard in different roles.

Even the comparatively ordinary international sides are so well organised today, most of them playing a variation of the Italian game. Well organised defences with plenty of men back, usually means frustration for England. This I think is because international football is based on a very different style of play compared with the English game at club level.

Every foreign team poses new problems and quite often by the time the England players have sorted out the strengths and weaknesses of the opposition the 90 minutes are up.

In any case I'm sure that given a little time, Don Revie will be able to create a successful England side. Over the years I played for him at Leeds I came to realise that he was the biggest factor in Leeds successes. Apart from his enormous capacity for hard work he has the happy knack of being able to pick out the right sort of players, sifting out the

Paul Madeley (right) says 'little fellows give me most trouble' . . . like Burnley's Leighton James (photo left). Above, Leeds' Frank Gray.

players who would be able to perform at top level.

With England, Don Revie is still a great manager with an uncanny knack of being able to inspire the players. There's something about him and his team talks, difficult to define exactly, but when he's finished talking all the players feel they want to go out and massacre the opposition just for him.

I've heard it suggested last season that Leeds United are over the hill and particularly with regard to Johnny Giles and Billy Bremner. I cannot see either of them being finished yet by a long way, but when the time does come, Eddie Gray and his younger brother Frank will go a long way towards filling the gaps they leave. Frank is still only 20 and was always a midfield player until he was switched to left back when Trevor Cherry was unavailable.

Then there's this fellow Duncan McKenzie who is terribly gifted and really unpredictable. I saw him produce a fantastic touch of magic with the ball in training in a one against one session. Against one of the young Leeds professionals, Duncan moved in front of the ball and somehow brought it

up his back and over his head, flicking it some twelve feet in the air and dropping it behind his opponent. The young lad just looked at him with his mouth open.

Duncan said 'I'm keeping it for a dry pitch' . . . but if he ever pulls that off in a game it'll be fantastic.

Leeds players are reknowned as a very superstitious lot. I think Don Revie started it, doing little things on match days and the players going out in a certain order, like the centre half in front of the goalkeeper and so on. I never was particularly superstitious myself though in a football sense I grew up in a very superstitious atmosphere. I wasn't affected so much as the other players because I rarely wore the same number for two games in a row. So of course I was always changing my position in the line as the players left the dressing room and went onto the pitch.

Personally I'm more concerned with realities than superstitions and I am happiest when my immediate opponent is a big fellow. I'm not slow on the run, but being big, it's the little fellows that have real pace and skilful control of the ball that can get past me. Probably the two players that give me most trouble are Leighton James of Burnley and Dave Thomas of Queens Park Rangers. They are both able to go either way and are very quick off the mark.

The Southern League side Wimbledon gave us a lot of trouble in the FA Cup last season but it was not really a surprise to me. There have always been surprises by lowly clubs in the Cup and there always will be. They couldn't sustain that peak form over a long league season, but non-League sides and clubs in lower divisions can raise their game for the big occasion.

In the First Division, Leeds, Liverpool and the Manchester clubs have taken the limelight for several years now but everything goes in cycles. Arsenal did the double of course, but apart from that the top honours have generally been dominated by northern clubs.

But it's just a matter of time before one of the southern clubs starts to put it all together and becomes a serious challenger again. Based on last season, the team I feel was most difficult to beat amongst the southern clubs was West Ham. They had been playing well before we played them each time last season and built up their confidence. I would expect them to show up well again this season . . . but Leeds will be thereabouts as well.

Ray Clemence of Liverpool foils Ipswich's Kevin Beattie on the line.

RALF EDSTRÖM

SWEDEN'S GIANT STRIKER

———— ★ ————

WHEN Ralf Edström first hit the headlines in Sweden it was largely due to his size and his heading ability. Standing 6 foot 5 inches and jumping well, he was almost unbeatable in the air. Other players with a similar build have shone briefly but failed to develop as all round players, but Edström has improved quite remarkably in the last three years.

It was Swedish Second Division club Degerfors that first discovered Edström, giving him a few league games in the 1970 season. He earned a place in Sweden's youth team and almost immediately had all the most ambitious clubs in Sweden after him.

Edström chose the little known club Atvidaberg, where he first teamed up with Roland Sandberg. Together these two were to spearhead Sweden's qualification for the 1974 World Cup and despite the limitations of the near-amateur Swedes, threw a fright into the West Germans whom they led 1–0 at half time when they met in the big competition. Even with 12 minutes left Sweden still held the Germans to 2–2 and Edström and Sandberg had scored the goals.

In Atvidaberg's 1972 league campaign, Edström earned a regular first team place, but still only 19 he started quietly. In the first half of the season he scored only two goals, then early in August he took a hat trick of headed goals against the Soviet Union in Stockholm and never looked back.

Ralf Edström (above) who burst onto the international scene with a hat-trick of headed goals for Sweden against Russia when he was only 20.

The Russians led 3–1 at half time in that match and finally managed a 4–4 draw, but they had no answer to Edström's ability in the air. Neither did Norway or Malta, Sweden's remaining opponents that year and Edström helped himself to another five international goals.

In the championship, Edström appeared to acquire a new confidence after his success against Russia. Lining up at centre forward or inside left, with Sandberg on the left wing, Edström hit 14 goals in the second half of the season. Atvidaberg took the championship for the first time ever, and Edström and Sandberg shared the First Division scorers crown with 16 goals each.

Edström's exploits repeatedly made headlines in the sports pages of Sweden's newspapers and somewhat prematurely, when still only 20 years old, he was voted 'Footballer of the Year'.

Swedish goalkeeper Ronnie Hellstroem (photo right) now plays for 1FC Kaiserslautern in West Germany.

Sweden has long been a popular hunting ground for scouts from professional clubs and inevitably Edström and Sandberg attracted attention from foreign clubs. Italians and Spaniards were interested but with their frontiers closed at that time, Sandberg went to West Germany and Edström signed for the Dutch club, PSV Eindhoven.

Just before he left, Edström starred in a 1–0 win over touring Brazil in Stockholm, but he returned to play in World Cup qualifying matches. Sweden

Roland Sandberg (below) on the right, jinks past an opponent. He and Edström played together in Sweden for Atvidaberg FF and were reunited in the World Cup.

Sweden's World Cup team manager Georg Ericsson (above) who brought back emigrant stars like Edström (right) and Ove Grahn (photo left) who plays in Switzerland.

were included in a group with Hungary and Austria and with half their team recalled from foreign clubs, finally qualified after beating Austria 2–1 in a play off at Gelsenkirchen.

With PSV, the sports club of the giant Phillips Electrical Company, Edström continued to score goals but also began to develop as an all-round player. Under the guidance of the PSV coach Kees Rijvers, Edström played as one of two central strikers, but left of centre.

In his first season in Holland, Edström played a major part in PSV's cup campaign which culminated in a 6–0 victory over NAC Breda in the final.

Then came the World Cup in which Edström teamed up again with Roland Sandberg, Ove Grahn from Switzerland and Bjorn Nordquist, his club colleague with PSV.

Sweden were not given much chance in a group that included Holland and Uruguay, but the South

Americans proved to be one of the biggest disappointments in the competition. Edström scored twice in a 3–0 win over Uruguay that clinched Sweden's passage into the second stage.

Playing with a well organised, physically strong defence, the hard-working Swedes beat Yugoslavia 2–1 with Edström again amongst the scorers and in a critical encounter, they dominated the first half of an exciting game with West Germany. Edström contributed one of Sweden's goals, a tremendous volley from a ball fed in from the right. On the edge of the German penalty area, Edström met the ball in the air with his left foot, hammered it over the bunch of players inside the area, and saw it dip late in flight, to flash under the bar beyond Maier's reach into the far corner corner of the net.

Edström's ability in the air and his powerful left foot are still his greatest weapons but he now uses both attributes in a variety of ways.

Surrounded by a group of very good Dutch players, Edström is a target for all manner of passes laid up to him, positioned deep in enemy territory. He nods down high crosses for colleagues to shoot; he beats opponents on the left and pulls passes back, predominantly for Dutch international Willy Van der Kuylen, coming from midfield . . . and still gets goals himself.

Early in the 1974–75 season it was clear that PSV were poised to challenge the ten year domination of the two Dutch giants, Ajax and Feyenoord. Entertaining Feyenoord, the reigning champions, early in the season, PSV beat them 3–2 with Edström scoring all three goals. Later in the season, with Edström wearing a specially designed plastic mask to protect a broken nose he had sustained a week earlier, PSV beat Feyenoord again 3–2 before a 65,000 crowd in Rotterdam. This was Feyenoord's first home defeat for four years.

Sweden's reserve bench in the World Cup (bottom left) and top left, West German stars Gerd Müller and Uli Hoeness attracting the photographers while they wait for the kick off. On the right, West Ham's Keith Robson sidesteps an opponent with a flick from his elegant and lethal left foot.

In the autumn of 1974, Edström declined an invitation to play for Sweden against Holland, presumably regarding PSV's championship bid to be more important. Later, his international colleagues in the Bundesliga demanded that the Swedish FA, pay for appearances and increase their win bonuses for foreign based players, which puts Edström's future international career in doubt.

His contract stipulates that PSV will release him for all competitive international games and still only 23 he seems certain to be one of the stars in the next World Cup. But whatever his international future, Edström and PSV Eindhoven are clearly going to be a power in the European game for some years, both in Holland and in international club competitions.

RUBEN AYALA
NEEDS AN ATTACKING TEAM
TO DEVELOP HIS POTENTIAL

By

Ubaldo Perez

♦   ♦   ♦

RUBEN Hugo Ayala first came into the European spotlight in October, 1972, when a game for charity was staged in Basle, Switzerland, between Europe and South America. Like most of these well intentioned representative matches, it flopped because club interests came first. South America won 2–0, Ayala figured on the right wing for the first half, then went off for a shower to give Peru's Baylon a run and then came back as a substitute on the left wing for the last ten minutes.

Not one British player took part and 9 of the South Americans who appeared were from Argen-

Ruben Ayala, Atletico Madrid's Argentina-born striker, has already proved his ability (portrait right). In the World Cup he showed he has the skill, pace and finishing power but needs an attack orientated team to support him. Photo left shows Ayala in a tussle with Brazil's Mario Marinho.

118

tina. The occasion was a flop in every sense with only 14,000 in attendance.

A year later, Ayala came back to Europe to play for Spanish champions Atletico Madrid, but first he was to spearhead Argentina's qualification for the World Cup. Ayala played in all four matches, at home and away to Paraguay and Bolivia and scoring 5 of Argentina's 9 goals. Perhaps the most vital was a fine left foot shot in Asuncion, when Paraguay were held to 1–1 away, but in the return game that Argentina had to win to qualify, Ayala scored twice (including one from a penalty) in a rough-house game. Tempers flared, players were sent off and the boots flew above waist height, but Argentina won 3–1.

In that summer of 1973, Ayala helped his club San Lorenzo de Almagro to the Argentinian championship. Then with his club manager, Juan Carlos Lorenzo having agreed to replace the Austrian, Max Merkel, in charge of Atletico Madrid, Ayala and his club mate Heredia followed Lorenzo to Spain after Argentina's qualifying matches were over.

Twenty three years old and with 14 internationals behind him, Ayala never quite reproduced his best form in Spain. First he was hampered by a string of niggling injuries that often kept him out of Atletico's team, but if his qualities were more European than South American, European tactics denied him the close support of colleagues in sufficient numbers.

Ayala is quick, very quick, with the technical skills to go past his man on either side. His style is direct and simple, straight for goal with his long hair flying in the wind, and he shoots powerfully with either foot. But too often he was called upon to drop back and work defensively, when his talents cry out for the freedom to go forward.

Ayala was unhappy in Spain, frequently asking to be transferred back to Argentina. In the semi-final of the European Cup against Celtic in Glasgow, he was the one player who could have created problems for the Scottish defenders but tragically, he fell victim to Lorenzo's defensive plans that included the systematic kicking of the Celtic forwards.

In a hysterical atmosphere on a wild night at Parkhead, half Ayala's colleagues should have been sent off in the first thirty minutes. Early in the second half, he committed a minor foul, and Dogan

World Cup action on the left. Upper photo shows Argentina's René Houseman in possession with Ayala (centre) making a break. Lower picture shows another Argentina star who made a big impact, Carlos Babington, dispossessing a Brazilian. Babington was to have joined Stoke City but his father let his British passport lapse. Photo right shows Ayala breaking—and when Ayala goes he shouts for a pass.

Babacan, the Turkish referee sent him off. The referee was technically correct, for Ayala had received a yellow card in the first half, but it was incredible and unjust that Ayala should be sent off while Panadero Diaz, the Atletico left back was blatantly committing atrocious fouls on Celtic's Jimmy Johnstone.

Ayala's second visit to Britain was with Argentina, rejoining his old colleagues for their pre-World Cup, warm up games. Against England at Wembley, Ayala proved to be a real handful, always easy to find, supremely gifted with the ball at his feet and in the modern manner getting his crosses in early.

Mario Kempes, the left footed centre forward scored both Argentina's goals in a 2–2 draw but it was Ayala who created the major problems for the England defence, involved in all their most menacing attacks.

In the World Cup, Ayala's qualities showed up once more but in most games he had insufficient support. In the 1–1 draw with Italy he was nominally the right winger, tight-marked by Facchetti whom he frequently turned both ways. He spent as much time on the left wing as he did on the right and whenever he got the ball he created problems for everyone.

Time after time, Ayala's combination of skill and irrepressible speed carried him into threatening positions but most of his efforts came to nothing. No matter how many men he beat, there were always defenders covering and invariably when Ayala needed close support to lay the ball off, or a colleague in the goalmouth for whom he could aim with a telling pass, the Argentinian attack was always short in numbers.

Another Argentinian who took the eye in the World Cup was Carlos Alberto Babington, a gifted penetrative inside forward. Together with Ayala, this pair could have added a new dimension to Argentinian football but like Brazil, they were always too cautious, consistently defensive in their outlook and more concerned in containing their opponents attack.

Photo right shows Ayala taking a break from training. On the left, Don Givens of Q.P.R. beats Derby's Archie Gemmill to a ball in the air.

Enrico Sivori, an outstanding, attacking inside forward in his time, had supervised Argentina's path through the qualifying stages. With his support and a team with an attacking posture, Ayala had thrived and it is conceivable that had Sivori not been replaced they would have played in a more positive, creative style.

True, the Argentinians were not guilty of the excesses that have marred their game whenever they have met European opponents in the past. But it was only when they found themselves 2–0 down to Poland that they really made a determined effort to attack. In Ayala, they had a spearhead, equally at home in the centre or on the right, who displayed the ability and pace to turn defenders, go past opponents and destroy their covering system.

Like all the best players, Ayala varies his game, frequently laying the ball off to a colleague with a deft touch and is gone like quicksilver. Given a good ball laid in front of him Ayala has the speed and finishing power to shine in any company and score goals. With and without the ball his presence is menacing and still only twenty five he could be a revelation if he were to find himself playing for a team with the emphasis on attack.

GOALKEEPERS NEED
COURAGE AND CONCENTRATION

BY

RAY CLEMENCE
of
Liverpool and England

I have heard it said that all goalkeepers are a bit mad–crazy is another word that's been used. But I don't see that at all. Certainly you can get kicked in the head going down for a ball at an opponents feet, particularly if you do it the wrong way, but forwards are just as liable to be injured going for diving headers in the goalmouth where feet are flashing around.

What goalkeepers really need today is courage and concentration. Courage, because there are situations where a goalkeeper would be lost if he wasn't a little courageous and concentration because these days, a goalkeeper may be called upon to make perhaps only two or three saves in an entire match. With so little to do in many games you really have to concentrate on staying alert.

Courage is not only needed in one against one

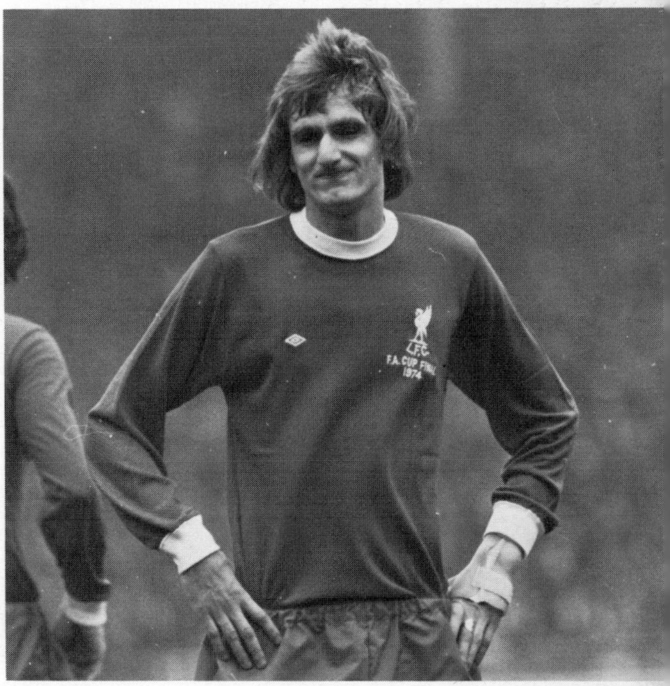

Liverpool goalkeeper Ray Clemence (photo left) says Emlyn Hughes and Phil Thompson (photo right) our twin toppers, like me to come out and help deal with high crosses.'

123

situations when an opponent has broken through and you have to go down at his feet. At corners and free kicks, penalty areas are so crowded these days it's often like Piccadilly Circus in the rush hour. It requires a certain kind of courage to keep your head in such crowded conditions.

Playing in goal can also be a very lonely occupation, particularly in a successful side like Liverpool. In most games you have so little to do that 90% of a goalkeeper's job is based on concentration. There must be dozens of very good goalkeepers all over the country for I see some of them in Sunday matches in local parks, making saves all over the place. But most of them, put in front of a big crowd

with nothing to do for half an hour maybe, and then called on to make a save in the last five minutes of a game, just couldn't do it because they would have been unable to concentrate.

Playing for England, concentration is perhaps even more important. The games I played in for England last season underline this, for against Czechoslovakia at Wembley I had to deal with only two shots in the entire match. And against Portugal a few weeks later I didn't have a shot at all.

Goalkeepers are very vulnerable at top level for in international matches these days it is extremely difficult to create chances. Where the continental score today is in my opinion, in their superior finishing.

In League games, most English teams will create seven or eight chances in a match and generally would say the forwards manage to turn only 50% of these chances into shots on target. The continental

Photo left, Italy's Dino Zoff, 'the only foreign 'keeper up to English standards,' says Clemence. Above, long-serving Liverpool stalwart Tommy Smith and photo right shows crowded area at Highbury with Mark Wallington of Leicester winning the ball from John Radford.

on the other hand, may create only two or three chances in a game but their superior finishing ability will enable them to get a shot on target almost every time. They may not score with every shot, but they usually call on the 'keeper to make a save.

With Liverpool always being involved in one of the big three European competitions I've been around a bit at club level too and I would say that amongst the best continental clubs the finishing is just as deadly. Red Star of Yugoslavia and the West Germans, Borussia Monchengladbach are probably the best examples.

When we played Red Star in Belgrade we weren't particularly impressed by them, but they put us out of the 1973-74 European Cup campaign with a great show at Anfield. As a team, they played some great possession stuff and they beat us 2–1 in Liverpool, in a match in which they had only two shots at goal . . . and both were fantastic efforts.

With Monchengladbach it was the other way around for we beat them quite easily in the first leg at Anfield 3–0. Then in Germany they played some really good football and were 2–0 up in the first twenty minutes and one of these goals was incredible.

Stoke City and former Chelsea star Alan Hudson (photo left) and above, Ray Clemence's chief rival for the England jersey, Hudson's club-mate Peter Shilton. Photo right is of Jovan Acimovic the midfield general of Red Star who put Liverpool out of the European Cup in 1973–74 with a great 2–1 win at Anfield.

It was scored by their left winger Jupp Heynckes who hit the ball from just outside the box with the inside of his right foot and the ball must have bent five or six yards in the air.

If the best of the continentals have the edge in finishing I'm sure that English goalkeepers leave the foreigners cold. The only continental goalkeeper that I would exempt from this general criticism is Dino Zoff of Italy and Juventus. The other foreign goalkeepers go out and punch too many crosses and knock down too many shots. In both situations the ball goes loose, perhaps to give someone else the chance to try another shot and it is in this aspect of the game that English goalkeepers are superior. On the whole the English 'keeper holds a very high proportion of crosses and shots and the danger is over with the ball in his arms.

This is particularly true of goalkeepers like Peter Shilton of Stoke City and Phil Parkes of Queens Park Rangers. And there's another one on the way up—West Ham's Mervyn Day who has really great potential.

Peter Shilton and I are great friends despite the fact that we are rivals in the England squad. On tour we always room together, and in training as well as in matches, we help each other all we can.

I got my first chance to play for England three years ago when Peter was unfit for the World Cup qualifying match against Wales. England won 1–0 and Sir Alf Ramsey kept the same team for the return game at Wembley. Then in 1974 Peter played in the three home internationals and the Wembley game against Argentina before Joe Mercer gave me the jersey for the game in East Germany. I stayed for the other tour matches in Yugoslavia and Bulgaria.

That's the nice thing about playing for England. There's a great atmosphere amongst the players and whoever is picked to play in goal can count on the complete support of the other 'keepers in the squad.

We've got the same kind of spirit in the Liverpool camp even though the personnel change over the years. The important thing is that every player helps everyone else and they complement each other.

Photo left, Ray Clemence in action. He can throw the ball almost as far as he can kick it.

For Liverpool I've played behind three sets of stoppers so far. My first half dozen games were behind Ron Yeats and Tommy Smith and then Larry Lloyd replaced Yeats to pair up with Tommy Smith. Playing behind either of these two pairs I couldn't get near anything in the air because they wanted to win every ball, and it was very, very rare that they missed anything.

Last season our twin stoppers were Phil Thompson and Emlyn Hughes and they like me to come out and help deal with high crosses. Previously I had only been called on to make reflex saves on the line, but playing a bigger part in the defensive set-up has made me a more complete goalkeeper.

Of course, goalkeeping is a specialised position and if courage and concentration are vital, it also helps to be thick skinned. If outfield players make mistakes they can compensate later and there's usually someone on hand to cover up in defence, but when a goalkeeper errs, he invariably pays for it with a goal. You have to be able to withstand criticism and often abuse from newspapers and television and shrug it off right away. If you dwell on your mistakes you're lost.

TV can also be an asset however, though it pinpoints goalkeeping errors more sharply and clearly than any other media. Sitting in the bath after a match in which you've conceded a goal in front of the cameras you can actually look forward to seeing it again. Without TV you can only rely on your memory when trying to re-assess a situation and your decision, but with TV you can think about a goal after the game, and say . . . 'yes I might have done this . . .' and then get a second look. This is of great advantage when a similar situation is presented to you in later matches. So television to me is a double-sided thing.

I had a nightmare debut for Liverpool in a League Cup game against Swansea that was played in a gale of a wind and pouring rain. We won 2–0 but I had one of those games in which it all goes wrong and my kicking in particular was terrible. One spectator at the Anfield Road end called out to me . . . 'Clemence, why don't you take an early shower?'

But the Liverpool fans are great, creating a tremendous atmosphere and perhaps the nicest thing . . . when you make mistakes, they are always quick to forgive you.

THE YEAR'S INTERNATIONAL
FOOTBALL

THE period under review includes matches played in the final stages of the 1974 World Championship won by the host country, West Germany, and largely dominated by European nations, and the first matches played in the qualifying competition for the European Football Championship, the final tournament (between the last four) of which will be staged in the summer of 1976.

It was in anticipation both of European successes in the 1974 World Championship and of the quickening interest in the European Football Championship that, with the exception of the pre-World Cup line-ups of Argentina and Brazil, I concentrated last year on the line-ups of European countries, particularly those in the same European Football Championship qualifying groups as the four British associations.

This year I have stayed entirely with the Europeans. Obviously those who took the top three places in the 1974 World Championship–West Germany, the Netherlands and Poland in that order; and also the three other European countries who qualified for the Second Round group matches–East Germany (the only country during the tournament to beat the eventual winners, West Germany), Sweden and Yugoslavia.

Two of the latter three had, incidentally, been First Round group *winners* but had failed to qualify either as Second Round Group winners to contest the Final, or as Second Round Group runners-up to contest the match to decide the third and fourth placings in the World Championship. Overall in fact in the eight Second Round matches played between First Round Group *winners* and First Round Group *runners-up*, one match was drawn, three won by 'winners' but four won by 'runners-up'.

Whether or not that proves that the reduction of the Knock-out element until the Final itself by the introduction of the league-system for the Second Round (instead of knock-out quarter-finals) does give a truer picture of merit, probably cannot be assessed on the basis of the results of this one tournament. It does suggest however that the change should be retained for the 1978 Championship.

However, whatever schemes men (even experienced football administrators) dream up, football remains 'a funny old game' and the forecasting of results as difficult at international level as it is at Football League level for all those of us who still dream of an early retirement thanks to the Pools!

It was on 16 January 1974 that UEFA met in Paris to 'draw' the groups for the qualifying competition of the European Football Championship. It was not a straightforward draw but a seeded one. The top seeds were placed in one category; the bottom seeds in another; and then, as a useful expedient, the rest divided into roughly the NATO (Western European) and the Warsaw Pact (East and Central European) countries.

The listing of the top and bottom seeds was done on the basis of performances in the qualifying competition for the previous European Football Championship when the respective qualifying groups were headed by Belgium, England, West Germany, Hungary, Italy, Rumania, the Soviet Union and Yugoslavia. Those eight were placed in the top seed category. In that previous competition the bottom clubs in the qualifying groups were Albania, Cyprus, Denmark, Finland, the Republic of Ireland, Luxembourg, Malta and Norway. Albania have not entered for the present competition but Iceland have and they, and the remaining seven bottom-placed countries from the previous competition, became the 'minnow' category.

The remaining sixteen entrants were neatly divided between the NATO combination of France, Greece, N. Ireland, the Netherlands, Portugal, Scotland, Turkey and Wales; and the mixed category of Soviet and neutral countries–Austria, Bulgaria, Czechoslovakia, East Germany, Poland, Spain, Sweden and Switzerland.

The draw was made by picking one country from each of those four categories to make each qualifying group. The system seems fair enough although it did mean using 1971 match results whereas there was already available to UEFA, the results of the 1973 European section of the World Championship qualifying competition. These matches had produced eight European qualifiers plus West Germany the host country. On the most recent form these had more entitlement to top seeding. Instead the EFC qualifying competition has three of its eight qualifying groups without a single 1974 World Cup finalist in it–Groups One, Two and Six.

In two of the qualifying groups (*with only one country from each group to go forward to the quarter finals*) two World Cup qualifiers are in opposition–West Germany and Bulgaria in Group 8; and, more unfortunately, Sweden and Yugoslavia in Group 3

(both of whom reached the last eight in the World Championship). But the most unfortunate of all the groups–and one that must seriously discredit any claim that the eight EFC group winners will be the top eight European countries on current form– is Group 5. Here Italy (a World Cup qualifier albeit very disappointing in the final tournament) were the top seed, and Finland the bottom ranker–and the two 'other' countries drawn from their categories were the Netherlands and Poland, the second and third countries in the 1974 Championship!

GORDON JEFFERY

(Unless indicated otherwise the line-ups are in 4–3–3 formation. WC stands for World Cup; BHC for British Home Championship; and EFC for European Football Championship)

N. IRELAND

A	11. 5. 74	N. Ireland....................1 (Cassidy)	Scotland 0	— Glasgow (BHC) (N.I. 'home' match)
B	15. 5. 74	England.....................1 (Weller)	N. Ireland...................0	— Wembley (BHC)
C	18. 5. 74	Wales.......................1 (Smallman)	N. Ireland...................0	— Wrexham (BHC)
D	4. 9. 74	Norway ....2 (Lund 2)	N. Ireland...................1 (Finney)	— Oslo (EFC)
E	30. 10. 74	Sweden 0	N. Ireland...................2 (Nicholl, O'Neill)	— Stockholm (EFC)

	A	B	C	D	E			A	B	C	D	E
Jennings......	G	G	G	G	G		Blair.........	—	—	—	—	LB[2]
Rice.........	RB	RB	RB	RB	—		Hamilton	RH[1]	RH	RH[1]	RH	RH
O'Kane......	RCB	RCB	RCB	RCB	RB		Cassidy	CH	CH	CH	CH	—
Nicholl.......	—	—	—	—	RCB		Clements......	LH	LH	LH	LH	—
Hunter.......	LCB	LCB	LCB	LCB	LCB		McIlroy.......	RF	RF	RF	CF	CF
Nelson.......	LB	LB[1]	—	—	LB[1]		Finney.......	—	—	—	RF	—
Jackson	RH[2]	LB[2]	RH[2]	—	CH		O'Neill........	—	—	CF	—	RF
Dowd........	—	—	LB	—	LH		Morgan.......	CF	CF	—	—	LF
Craig........	—	—	—	LB	—		McGrath......	LF	LF	LF	LF	

POLAND

A	17. 4. 74	Belgium.....................1 (Van Moer)	Poland......................1 (Deyna)	— Liege
B	15. 5. 74	Poland......................2 (Lato, Jacobczak)	Greece......................0	— Warsaw
C	15. 6. 74	Poland......................3 (Lato 2, Szarmach)	Argentina ....2 (Heredia, Babington)	— Stuttgart (WC)
D	19. 6. 74	Poland......................7 (Szarmach 3, Lato 2, Deyna, Gorgon)	Haiti 0	— Munich (WC)

	A	B	C	D	E	F	G	H	I	J	K	L	M	N	O
Kalinowski	G	G^2	—	—	—	—	—	—	—	—	—	—	—	—	—
Fischer	—	G^1	—	—	—	—	—	—	—	—	—	—	—	—	—
Tomaszewski	—	—	G	G	G	G	G	G	G	G	G	G	—	—	G
Mowlik	—	—	—	—	—	—	—	—	—	—	—	—	—	G^1	—
Karwecki	—	—	—	—	—	—	—	—	—	—	—	—	—	G^2	—
Gut	RB	—	—	LCB^2	—	LB	—	—	—	—	—	—	—	—	—
Bulzacki	LCB	RB^1	—	—	—	—	—	—	—	LB	LCB	LCB^1	—	—	—
Sobczynski	—	RB^2	—	—	—	—	—	—	—	LB^2	LCB^2	—	—	LB^1	—
Szymanowski	—	—	RB	RB	RB	RB	RB	RB	RB	RB	RB	RB	RB	—	RB
Wawrowski	—	—	—	—	—	—	—	—	—	—	—	—	—	RB	—
Cmikiewcz	RCB	—	LF^2	LH^2	CF^2	—	CF^2	LH^2	RH^2	LH	LH	LH^1	—	—	—
Gorgon	—	RCB	RCB	RCB	RCB	RCB	RCB	RCB	RCB	RCB	RCB^1	—	—	—	RCB
Kopicera	—	—	—	—	—	—	—	—	—	—	RCB^2	RH	—	—	—
Wieczorek	—	—	—	—	—	—	—	—	—	—	—	RCB	—	RCB	—
Ostafinski	—	—	—	—	—	—	—	—	—	—	—	—	RCB	—	—
Zmuda	—	LCB	LB	LB	LB	LCB	LCB	LCB	LCB	—	—	—	—	—	—
Musial	LB	LB	LCB	LCB^1	LCB	—	LB	LB	LB	LCB	LB^1	—	—	—	—
Wyrobek	—	—	—	—	—	—	—	—	—	—	—	—	LCB	—	LCB
Maculewicz	—	—	—	—	—	—	—	—	—	—	—	—	—	LCB	—
Drzewiecki	—	—	—	—	—	—	—	—	—	—	LB	LB	—	—	LB
Rudy	—	—	—	—	—	—	—	—	—	—	—	—	—	LB^2	—
Kasperczak	RH	CH	RH	RH	RH	RH	RH	RH^1	RH^1	CH^1	—	—	RH^1	—	—
Garlowski	—	RH^1	—	—	—	—	—	—	—	—	—	—	—	CH	—
Kmiecik	—	RH^2	—	—	—	CF^2	—	RH^2	—	—	—	—	—	—	—
Jacobczak	—	LH	—	—	—	—	—	—	—	—	RH^2	—	—	LH^1	—
Kasalik	—	—	—	—	—	—	—	—	—	—	—	—	—	RH	—
Deyna	CH	—	CH	CH	CH	CH^1	CH	CH	—	CH	CH	CH	—	—	CH
Maszczyk	LH	—	LH	LH^1	LH	LH	LH	LH^1	LH	RH	RH	LH^2	—	—	RH
Bula	—	—	—	—	—	—	—	—	—	—	—	LH	—	—	LH
Kasperski	—	—	—	—	—	—	—	—	—	—	—	—	LH^2	—	—
Lato	RF	RF^1	RF	RF	RF	RF	RF	RF	RF	RF	RF	RF	RF	—	RF
Kusto	—	RF^2	—	—	—	—	—	—	CH^2	—	CF^2	—	—	—	—
Domarski	CF^1	CF^1	CF^2	—	—	—	CH^2	CF	—	—	—	—	—	—	—
Chojnacki	CF^2	—	—	—	—	—	—	—	—	—	—	—	—	RF	—
Kapka	—	CF^2	—	—	—	—	—	CF^2	—	CF^2	CF^1	—	—	—	—
Szarmach	—	—	CF^1	CF	CF^1	CF^1	CF^1	—	CF^1	CF	CF^1	—	CF^1	CF^1	CF
Marks	—	—	—	—	—	—	—	—	—	—	CF^2	—	—	—	—
Szpakowski	—	—	—	—	—	—	—	—	—	—	—	—	—	CF^2	—
Gadocha	LF	LF	LF^1	LF	LF	LF	LF	LF	LF	LF	LF	LF	LF	—	LF
Kwiatkowski	—	—	—	—	—	—	—	—	—	—	—	—	—	LF	—

BELGIUM

A	13. 3. 74	East Germany 1	Belgium 0	— E. Berlin
		(Streich)		
B	17. 4. 74	Belgium 1	Poland 1	— Liege
		(Van Moer)	(Deyna)	
C	1. 5. 74	Switzerland 0	Belgium 1	— Geneva
			(Van Herp)	
D	1. 6. 74	Belgium 2	Scotland 1	— Brussels
		(Henrotay, Lambert)	(Johnstone)	
E	8. 9. 74	Iceland 0	Belgium 2	— Rekjavik (EFC)
			(Van Moer 2)	
F	12. 10. 74	Belgium 2	France 1	— Brussels (EFC)
		(Martens, Van der Elst)	(Coste)	
G	7. 12. 74	East Germany 0	Belgium 0	— Leipzig (EFC)

	A	B	C	D	E	F	G
Piot	G	G	G	G	G	G	G
Van Binst	RB	RB	RB	RB	RB	RB	RB
Van den Daele	RCB	LCB	LCB	LCB	LCB	LCB	LCB
Dewalque	—	RCB	RCB	RCB[1]	—	—	CH
Broos	LCB	—	—	—	RCB	RCB	RCB
Martens	LB	LH	LB	LB	—	LB	LB
Thissen	—	LB	—	RCB[2]	—	—	—
Coeck	—	—	—	—	LB[1]	—	—
Cools	—	—	—	LF[2]	LB[2]	—	LH
Dockx	RH	LF[2]	RH[2]	—	—	LH[2]	—
Van Moer	CF[2]	RH[1]	CH	CH	CH	CH	—
Nicolas	LF[2]	RH[2]	—	—	—	—	—
Verheyen	CH	CH	RH[1]	RH	RH	RH	RH
Van Himst	LH	LF[1]	LH	LH	LH	LH[1]	RF[1]
Van der Elst	RF	—	—	—	RF	RF	RF[2]
Henrotay	—	RF	LF	LF[1]	LF	—	—
Van Herp	—	—	RF	RF	—	—	—
Devrindt	CF[1]	—	—	—	—	—	—
Lambert	—	CF	CF	CF	—	CF	CF
Teugels	—	—	—	—	CF[2]	LF	LF
Janssens	—	—	—	—	CF[1]	—	—
Nicolay	LF[1]	—	—	—	—	—	—

NORWAY

A	23. 5. 74	East Germany 1	Norway 0	— Rostock
		(Sparwasser)		
B	6. 6. 74	Norway 1	Scotland 2	— Oslo
		(Lund)	(Jordan, Dalglish)	
C	8. 8. 74	Sweden 2	Norway 1	— Gothenburg
		(Fredriksson, Tapper)	(Hestad)	
D	15. 8. 74	Norway 1	Finland 2	— Oslo
		(T. E. Johansen)	(Heiskanen, Paatelainen)	
E	4. 9. 74	Norway 2	N. Ireland 1	— Oslo (EFC)
		(Lund 2)	(Finney)	
F	30. 10. 74	Yugoslavia 3	Norway 1	— Belgrade (EFC)
		(Vukotic, Katalinski 2)	(Lund)	

	A	B	C	D	E	F
G. Karlsen	G	G	G	—	G	G
Thun	—	—	—	G	—	—
Wormdal	RB	RB	—	—	—	RB
Slinning	—	—	RB	LB	—	—
H. Karlsen	—	—	—	RB	—	—
Goa	—	—	—	—	RB	—
Birkelund	RCB	RCB	RCB	—	RCB	RCB
Brakstad	—	—	—	RCB	LCB	LCB
Kordahl	LCB	LCB	LCB	—	—	—
Grondalen	LB	LB	LB	LCB	LB	LB
Berg	RH	RH[1]	—	—	—	—

	A	B	C	D	E	F
Thunsberg	—	RH[2]	LH[1]	—	—	—
Valen	—	—	RH	RH	—	—
Austboe	—	—	—	—	RH	RH
T. E. Johansen	CH	CH	—	CH	CH	LH
Kvia	LH	LH	CH	LH	LH	CH[1]
Höyland	—	—	—	LH[2]	—	—
Skuseth	RF	RF	RF	—	—	—
Olsen	—	—	—	RF	—	RF
Lund	CF	CF	CF	—	CF	CF
Fuglset	—	—	—	CF	RF	CH[2]
Hestad	LF	LF	LF	LF	LF	LF

DENMARK

	A	B	C	D	E	F	G	H
B. Jensen	G	G	G	—	—	—	—	—
P. Poulsen	—	—	—	G	G	—	—	—
B. Larsen	—	—	—	—	—	G	G	G
Ahlberg	RB	RB	—	—	—	—	—	—
M. Olsen	—	—	RB	RH¹	LB	CH	CH	—
Mortensen	—	—	LB	RB	RB	RB	—	RB
Raaby	—	—	—	—	—	—	RB	—
S. Andersen	RCB¹	RCB	—	—	—	—	—	—
Toft	RCB²	—	—	—	—	—	—	—
L. Larsen	—	—	RCB	RCB	—	—	—	—
H. M. Jensen	—	—	—	—	RCB	RCB	RCB	RCB
Vonsyld	LCB	LCB	RH	LCB	LCB	—	—	—
Rasmusen	—	—	LCB	LB	—	LB	LB	LB
Seneca	—	—	CH	LH	CH	LCB	—	—
N. Sorensen	—	—	—	—	—	—	LCB²	—
S. Larsen	LB	LB	—	—	—	—	—	—
Ziegler	RH	RH²	—	—	—	—	—	—
H. E. Hansen	CH¹	RH¹	—	—	—	—	—	—
Jorgensen	LH²	CH²	—	RH²	—	RH²	—	CH
A. Sorensen	RF¹	RF¹	—	—	RH	RH¹	LCB¹	—
Danielsen	—	—	—	—	—	—	RH	LCB
J. S. Olsen	—	—	—	—	—	—	—	RH
J. Hansen	LH¹	CH¹	—	—	—	—	—	—
H. Hansen	CF	CF	LH	CH	—	—	—	—
Skovbö	LF	LH	—	—	—	—	—	—
Nygaard	—	—	—	—	LH	LH	—	—
Le Fevre	—	—	—	—	—	—	LH¹	LH
Skouborg	—	—	—	—	—	—	LH²	—
Nörregaard	RF²	LF²	—	—	—	—	—	—
Höiland	—	RF²	—	—	—	—	—	—
Lund	—	—	RF	RF¹	—	—	RF	RF
J. Pettersson	—	—	—	RF²	—	—	—	—
Simonsen	—	—	—	—	RF¹	RF	—	—
B. Pettersson	CH²	LF¹	—	CF	RF²	—	—	—
Aabech	—	—	CF	—	—	—	—	—
H. Jensen	—	—	—	—	CF	CF	—	—
Nielsen	—	—	—	—	—	—	CF	LF
Holmström	—	—	LF	LF	LF	LF¹	LF	CF
Flindt Bjerg	—	—	—	—	—	LF²	—	—

CZECHOSLOVAKIA

A 27. 3. 74 East Germany.............1 Czechoslovakia.............0 — Dresden
(Streich)

B 7. 4. 74 Brazil...................1 Czechoslovakia.............0 — Rio
(F. Marinho)

C 13. 4. 74 Bulgaria................0 Czechoslovakia.............1 — Plovdiv
(Dobias)

D 27. 4. 74 Czechoslovakia.............3 France...................3 — Prague
(Pivarnik, Bicovsky, Panenka) (Chiesa, Lacombe 2)

E 20. 5. 74 Soviet Union..............0 Czechoslovakia.............1 — Odessa
(Nehoda)

F 25. 9. 74 Czechoslovakia.............3 East Germany.............1 — Prague
(Bicovsky 2, Ondrus) (Hoffmann)

G 13. 10. 74 Czechoslovakia.............4 Sweden ....0 — Bratislava
(Svehlik 2, Masny, Bicovsky)

H 30. 10. 74 England..................3 Czechoslovakia.............0 — Wembley (EFC)
(Channon, Bell 2)

I 13. 11. 74 Czechoslovakia.............2 Poland...................2 — Prague
(Svehlik, Masny) (Gadocha, Szarmach)

J 20. 12. 74 Iran.....................0 Czechoslovakia.............1 — Teheran
(Ondrus)

	A	B	C	D	E	F	G	H	I	J
Viktor	G	—	—	—	G^1	G	G^2	G	G	—
Vencel	—	G	G	G	G^2	—	G^1	—	—	—
Cepo	—	—	—	—	—	—	—	—	—	G
Pivarnik	RB	RB	RB	RB	RB	RB^1	—	RB	RB^1	—
Dobias	CH^2	—	RCB	RCB	RCB	—	RB	—	—	—
Biros	—	—	—	—	—	—	—	—	RB^2	RB
Samek	RCB	RCB^1	—	—	—	—	—	—	—	—
Vojacek	—	RCB^2	—	—	CH^2	RCB^2	—	LCB^2	—	—
Jos. Capkovic	—	—	—	—	—	RCB^1	LCB	LCB^1	LCB	—
Ondrus	LCB	LCB	LCB	LCB	LCB	LCB	RCB	RCB	RCB	RCB
K. Gogh	—	—	—	—	—	—	—	—	—	LCB
Bendl	LB	LB	LB	—	—	—	—	—	—	—
Rygel	—	—	—	LB	LB	RB^2	—	—	—	—
Varadin	—	—	—	—	—	LB	LB	LB	LB	LB
Bicovsky	RH	CH	CH^2	RH^1	RH	CH	RH	RH^1	RH	CH
Kuna	—	RH	—	CH	CH^1	—	—	RH^2	—	—
Pekarik	CH^1	—	RH	—	CF^2	RH	CH	CH	CH^1	—
Cermak	—	—	—	RH^2	CF^1	—	—	—	—	—
I. Novak	—	—	CH^1	—	—	—	—	—	—	—
Knapp	—	—	—	—	—	—	—	—	CH^2	—
Gajdusek	LH^1	LH^1	LH^2	—	—	LH	LH	LH	LH	—
Panenka	LH^2	LH^2	LH^1	LH	LH	—	—	—	—	RH
Medvid	—	—	—	—	—	—	—	—	—	LH
Masrna	RF^1	—	—	—	—	—	—	—	—	—
B. Vesely	RF^2	RF	RF	RF	—	—	—	—	—	—
Svehlik	—	—	—	CF	RF^1	CF	CF^1	CF	CF	CF
Jarkovsky	—	LF	CF^2	—	RF^2	—	—	—	—	—
Masny	—	—	—	—	—	RF	RF	RF	RF	RF^1
Kroupa	—	—	—	—	—	CF^2	—	—	—	RF^2
Klement	LF^2	—	CF^1	—	—	—	—	—	—	—
Jan Capkovic	LF^1	—	—	—	—	—	—	—	—	LF
Petras	—	—	—	—	—	LF^1	—	—	—	—
Stratil	—	—	—	—	—	LF^2	LF	LF	LF	—
Nehoda	CF	CF	LF	LF	LF	—	—	—	—	—

ENGLAND

A	3. 4. 74	Portugal.................0	England....................0	—	Lisbon
B	11. 5. 74	Wales...................0	England....................2 (Bowles, Keegan)	—	Cardiff (BHC)
C	15. 5. 74	England.................1 (Weller)	N. Ireland................0	—	Wembley (BHC)
D	18. 5. 74	Scotland.................2 (Pejic o.g., Todd o.g.)	England....................0	—	Glasgow (BHC)
E	22. 5. 74	England.................2 (Channon, Worthington)	Argentina.................2 (Kempes 2)	—	Wembley
F	29. 5. 74	East Germany.............1 (Streich)	England....................1 (Channon)	—	Leipzig
G	1. 6. 74	Bulgaria.................0	England....................1 (Worthington)	—	Sofia
H	5. 6. 74	Yugoslavia...............2 (Petkovic, Oblak)	England....................2 (Channon, Keegan)	—	Belgrade
I	30. 10. 74	England.................3 (Channon, Bell 2)	Czechoslovakia............0	—	Wembley (EFC)
J	20. 11. 74	England.................0	Portugal...................0	—	Wembley (EFC)

	A	B	C	D	E	F	G	H	I	J
Parkes (QPR)	G	—	—	—	—	—	—	—	—	—
Shilton	—	G	G	G	G	—	—	—	—	—
Clemence	—	—	—	—	—	G	G	G	G	G
Nish	RB	RB	RB	RB	—	—	—	—	—	—
Hughes	—	LH	LH	LH	RB	RB	RB	RB	LB	LCB
Madeley	—	—	—	—	—	—	—	—	RB	RB
Todd	RCB	RCB	RCB	RCB	RCB	RCB	RCB	RCB	—	LB²
Watson	LCB	—	LCB²	LCB	LCB	LCB	LCB	LCB	RCB	RCB
McFarland	—	LCB	LCB¹	—	—	—	—	—	—	—
Hunter	—	—	LCB²	LCB¹	—	—	—	—	LCB	—
Pejic	LB	LB	LB	LB	—	—	—	—	—	—
Lindsay	—	—	—	—	LB	LB	LB	LB	—	—
Cooper	—	—	—	—	—	—	—	—	—	LB¹
Dobson	RH	—	—	—	RH	RH	RH	RH¹	—	—
Weller	—	RH	RH	RH	RH	—	—	—	—	—
Brooking	CH	—	—	—	LH	LH	LH	LH	RH²	RH
Bell	—	CH	CH	CH	CH	CH	CH	CH	CH	CH
Peters	LH	—	—	LF	—	—	—	—	—	—
G. Francis	—	—	—	—	—	—	—	—	LH	LH
Bowles	RF	CF	CF¹	—	—	—	—	—	—	—
Keegan	—	RF	RF	—	RF	RF	RF	RF	RF	—
Channon	LF	LF	LF	RF	LF	LF	LF	LF	LF	LF
Thomas	—	—	—	—	—	—	—	—	CF²	RF
Macdonald	CF¹	—	—	CF²	—	—	—	CF²	—	—
Ball	CF²	—	—	—	—	—	—	—	—	—
Worthington	—	—	CF²	CF¹	CF	CF	CF	CF¹	CF¹	CF²
Clarke	—	—	—	—	—	—	—	—	—	CF¹

ICELAND

A	19. 8. 74	Iceland...................2 (Hallgrimsson 2)	Finland....................2 (Paatelainen, Laine)	—	Reykjavik
B	8. 9. 74	Iceland...................0	Belgium....................2 (Van Moer 2)	—	Reykjavik (EFC)
C	9. 10. 74	Denmark..................2 (Lund, Le Fevre)	Iceland....................1 (Hallgrimsson)	—	Aalbourg
D	12. 10. 74	East Germany.............1 (Hoffmann)	Iceland....................1 (Hallgrimsson)	—	Magdeburg (EFC)

	A	B	C	D			A	B	C	D
Olafsson	G	G	G	G		A. Sigurvinsson	RH	RH	RH	RH
Thorsteinsson	RB	—	CH¹	RB²		Magnusson	CH	CH	CH²	CH
Torafsson	—	RB	RB	RB¹		Leifsson	LH	LH	LH	LH
A. Gunnarsson	RCB	—	—	—		Thordarsson	RF	—	RF	RF¹
Edvaldsson	—	RCB	RCB	RCB		Hedinsson	—	RF	—	RF²
Kjartansson	LCB	LCB	—	—		Hallgrimsson	CF	CF	CF	CF
Petursson	—	—	LCB	LCB		Eliasson	LF	LF	LF	LF
M. Geirsson	LB	LB	LB	LB						

EAST GERMANY

A 26. 2. 74 Tunisia .... 0 East Germany .... 4 — Tunis
(Lauck 2, Dorner, Frenzel)

B 28. 2. 74 Algeria. .... 1 East Germany .... 3 — Algiers
(Griche) (Streich, Matoul, Lowe)

C 13. 3. 74 East Germany .... 1 Belgium .... 0 — East Berlin
(Streich)

D 27. 3. 74 East Germany .... 1 Czechoslovakia .... 0 — Dresden
(Streich)

E 23. 5. 74 East Germany .... 1 Norway .... 0 — Rostock
(Sparwasser)

F 29. 5. 74 East Germany .... 1 England .... 1 — Leipzig
(Streich) (Channon)

G 14. 6. 74 East Germany .... 2 Australia .... 0 — Hamburg (WC)
(Curran o.g., Streich)

H 18. 6. 74 East Germany .... 1 Chile .... 1 — W. Berlin (WC)
(Hoffmann) (Ahumada)

I 22. 6. 74 West Germany .... 0 East Germany .... 1 — Hamburg (WC)
(Sparwasser)

J 26. 6. 74 East Germany .... 0 Brazil .... 1 — Hanover (WC)
(Rivelino)

K 30. 6. 74 East Germany .... 0 Netherlands. .... 2 — Gelsenkirchen (WC)
(Neeskens, Rensenbrink)

L 3. 7. 74 East Germany .... 1 Argentina .... 1 — Gelsenkirchen (WC)
(Streich) (Houseman)

M 4. 9. 74 Poland .... 1 East Germany .... 3 — Warsaw
(Lato) (Kurbjuweit, Vogel, Dorner)

N 25. 9. 74 Czechoslovakia .... 3 East Germany .... 1 — Prague
(Bicovsky 2, Ondrus) (Hoffmann)

O 9. 10. 74 East Germany .... 2 Canada .... 0 — Frankfurt/Oder
(Hoffmann, Dorner)

P 12. 10. 74 East Germany .... 1 Iceland .... 1 — Magdeburg (EFC)
(Hoffmann) (Hallgrimsson)

Q 30. 10. 74 Scotland .... 3 East Germany .... 0 — Glasgow
(Hutchison, Burns, Dalglish)

R 16. 11. 74 France .... 2 East Germany .... 2 — Paris (EFC)
(Guillou, Gallice) (Sparwasser, Kreische)

S 7. 12. 74 East Germany .... 0 Belgium .... 0 — Leipzig (EFC)

	A	B	C	D	E	F	G	H	I	J	K	L	M	N	O	P	Q	R*	S
Croy	G¹	G	G	G	G	G	G	G	G	G	G	G	G	G	—	G	G	G	G
Blochwitz	G²	—	—	—	—	—	—	—	—	—	—	—	—	—	—	—	—	—	—
Schulze	—	—	—	—	—	—	—	—	—	—	—	—	—	—	G	—	—	—	—
Fritsche	RB	—	RB¹	—	—	RB	—	—	—	—	—	—	—	—	—	—	—	—	—
Kurbjuweit	LB¹	RB	LB	RB	LB¹	—	—	LB	RB	LB	RB	CH	RH	RH²	LH	RH¹	RH	CH	CH
Watzlich	LB²	LB	RB²	LB	LB²	LB	—	LB	LB	LH	LB	—	—	LB	LB¹	LB	LB	LB	LB¹
Kische	—	—	—	RB	—	RB	RB	RB	LH	RB	LB	RCB	RB	RB	—	RB	RB	RB	RB
Bransch	RCB	RCB	RCB	RCB	RCB	RCB	RCB	RCB	RCB	RCB	RCB	RCB	RB	RCB	RCB	RB	RCB¹	—	—
Zapf	—	—	—	—	—	—	—	—	—	—	—	—	—	—	—	—	—	RCB	RCB²
Dorner	LH	LH	—	RH²	—	—	—	—	—	—	RH	CH	LH²	LB²	—	—	—	RCB	RCB
Weise	LCB	LCB	LCB	LCB	LCB	LCB	LCB	LCB	LCB	LCB	LCB	LCB	LCB	LCB	LCB	LCB	LCB	LCB	LCB
Decker	—	—	—	—	—	—	—	—	—	—	—	—	—	LB	CH	RH	—	—	—
Lauck	RH	CH	RH	RH¹	CH	—	—	RF	RH¹	LH¹	—	—	—	—	—	CH¹	—	RCH	LH
Seguin	—	RH¹	—	—	—	—	—	CH¹	—	—	—	—	—	RH¹	—	—	—	LCH²	—
Frenzel	CH¹	RH²	—	—	—	—	—	—	—	—	—	—	—	—	—	—	—	—	—
Irmscher	—	—	—	CH	RH	CH	RH	RH	RH¹	CH²	—	—	—	LH²	—	—	RH²	—	—
Pommerenke	—	—	—	—	RH	CH	—	—	—	RH	RH	—	LF²	LH¹	CH¹	—	—	—	—
Hamann	—	—	—	—	—	—	—	RH²	CH¹	—	—	—	—	—	—	—	—	—	—
Haefner	—	—	—	—	—	—	—	—	—	—	—	—	—	—	—	—	RF	LH	RH
Schnuphase	—	—	CH	LH	—	—	—	—	—	—	CH	CH	—	—	—	—	—	—	—
Kreische	—	—	—	—	LF²	LH	—	—	CH²	CH	—	LH²	—	—	—	—	LH	LCH¹	LB²
Sparwasser	CH²	LF²	LH	CF²	CF²	LH	LH	LH	CF	LF	LF	CF	LH	—	LH¹	—	CF	RF	—
Tyll	—	—	—	—	—	—	—	—	—	—	—	—	LH	—	—	—	—	—	—
Lowe	—	RF	RF	—	RF²	RF¹	RF	RF¹	—	—	RH²	RF¹	RF¹	—	—	—	—	—	—
Streich	CF¹	CF¹	RF	RF¹	LF	CF	CF	CF	—	CF	—	CF¹	CF²	CF²	CF	RF	CH²	—	CF
Hoffmann	—	—	—	RF²	LF²	RF²	RF	RF	CF	CF	RF	LF	RF	RF	RF	LF	LF	LF	RF
P. Ducke	—	—	—	CF¹	—	—	—	LF²	—	—	RF²	CF²	—	—	CF	—	—	—	—
Vogel	CF²	CF²	LF	LF¹	—	LF¹	LF	LF¹	—	—	RF²	LF	LF¹	LF¹	CH²	—	—	—	LF
Matoul	LF	LF¹	CF	—	—	—	—	—	—	—	—	—	—	—	—	—	—	—	—
Riedel	—	—	—	CF¹	—	—	—	—	—	—	—	—	—	—	—	—	—	—	—
Schellenberg	—	—	—	—	—	—	—	—	—	—	—	—	—	—	—	CF¹	CF¹	LF²	—

*4–4–2

WEST GERMANY

A 23. 2. 74 Spain .... 1 West Germany .... 0 — Barcelona
    (Asensi)
B 26. 2. 74 Italy .... 0 West Germany .... 0 — Rome
C 27. 3. 74 West Germany .... 2 Scotland .... 1 — Frankfurt
    (Breitner, Grabowski) (Dalglish)
D 17. 4. 74 West Germany .... 5 Hungary .... 0 — Dortmund
    (Muller 2, Wimmer, Holzenbein, E. Kremers)
E 1. 5. 74 West Germany .... 2 Sweden .... 0 — Hamburg
    (Hoeness, Heynckes)
F 14. 6. 74 West Germany .... 1 Chile .... 0 — W. Berlin (WC)
    (Breitner)
G 18. 6. 74 West Germany .... 3 Australia .... 0 — Hamburg (WC)
    (Overath, Cullmann, Muller)
H 22. 6. 74 West Germany .... 0 East Germany .... 1 — Hamburg (WC)
    (Sparwasser)
I 26. 6. 74 West Germany .... 2 Yugoslavia .... 0 — Dusseldorf (WC)
    (Breitner, Muller)
J 30. 6. 74 West Germany .... 4 Sweden .... 2 — Dusseldorf (WC)
    (Overath, Bonhof, Grabowski, Hoeness) (Edström, Sandberg)
K 3. 7. 74 West Germany .... 1 Poland .... 0 — Frankfurt (WC)
    (Muller)
L 7. 7. 74 West Germany .... 2 Netherlands .... 1 — Munich (WORLD CUP FINAL)
    (Breitner, Muller) (Neeskens)
M 4. 9. 74 Switzerland .... 1 West Germany .... 2 — Basle
    (Muller) (Cullmann, Geye)
N 20. 11. 74 Greece .... 2 West Germany .... 2 — Athens (EFC)
    (Delikaris, Eleftherakis) (Cullmann, Wimmer)
O 22. 12. 74 Malta .... 0 West Germany .... 1 — Valetta (EFC)
    (Cullmann)

	A	B	C	D	E	F	G	H	I	J	K	L	M	N	O
Maier	—	G	G	—	G	G	G	G	G	G	G	G	G	G	—
Nigbur	G	—	—	G	—	—	—	—	—	—	—	—	—	—	G
Vogts	RB^1	—	RB	RB	RB	RB	RB	RB	RB	RB	RB	RB	RB	RB	RB
Hottges	LB	RB^1	—	—	—	—	—	RCB^2	—	—	—	—	—	—	—
H. Kremers	LH^1	RB^2	—	LB	—	—	—	—	—	—	—	—	LB	LB	—
Weber	RCB	—	—	—	—	—	—	—	—	—	—	—	—	—	—
Schwarzenbeck	—	RCB	RCB	RCB^1	RCB	RCB	RCB	RCB^1	RCB	RCB	RCB	RCB	RCB^1	RCB	—
Korbel	—	—	—	—	—	—	—	—	—	—	—	—	—	—	RCB
Beckenbauer	LCB	LCB	LCB	LCB	LCB	LCB	LCB	LCB	LCB	LCB	LCB	LCB	LCB	LCB	LCB
Breitner	RB^2	LB	LB	—	LB	LB	LB	LB	LB	LB	LB	LB	—	—	—
Dietz	—	—	—	—	—	—	—	—	—	—	—	—	—	—	LB
Hoeness	RH	RF	CH	CH^1	CH	LH	LH	LH	LH^2	LH	LH	LH	RH	RH	—
Overath	CH	RH	—	—	—	CH^1	CH	CH^1	CH	CH	CH	CH	—	—	—
Cullmann	—	CH	RH	LH	RH^1	RH	RH^1	RH	—	—	—	—	LH	LH^1	LH^1
Wimmer	LH^2	—	LH	RH^1	—	—	RH^2	—	LH^1	—	—	—	—	CH	—
Holzenbein	—	—	—	RH^2	RH^2	CH^2	LF^2	—	RF^1	RF^1	LF	LF	CF^1	CF	LF
Bonhof	—	—	—	RCB^2	LF^3	—	—	—	RH	RH	RH	RH	CH	—	RH
Flohe	—	—	—	CH^2	—	—	—	LF	RF^2	RF^2	—	—	—	—	CH
Netzer	—	LH	—	—	LH	—	—	CH^2	—	—	—	—	—	—	—
Kapellmann	—	—	—	—	—	—	—	—	—	—	—	—	RCB^2	LH^2	—
Selinger	—	—	—	—	—	—	—	—	—	—	—	—	—	—	LH^2
Grabowski	RF^1	—	RF	RF	RF	RF	RF	RF	—	LF^2	RF	RF	—	—	—
Heynckes	RF^2	LF	—	—	LF^2	LF	LF^1	—	—	—	—	—	—	LF^1	—
Geye	—	—	—	—	—	—	—	—	—	—	—	—	RF	RF	—
Pirrung	—	—	—	—	—	—	—	—	—	—	—	—	—	LF^2	RF^1
Nickel	—	—	—	—	—	—	—	—	—	—	—	—	—	—	RF^2
Muller	CF	CF	CF	CF	CF	CF	CF	CF	CF	CF	CF	CF	—	—	—
Seel	—	—	—	—	—	—	—	—	—	—	—	—	CF^2	—	—
Kostedde	—	—	—	—	—	—	—	—	—	—	—	—	—	—	CF
Herzog	LF	—	LF	—	—	—	—	—	LF	LF^1	—	—	LF	—	—
E. Kremers	—	—	—	LF	LF^1	—	—	—	—	—	—	—	—	—	—

ITALY

A 26. 2. 74 Italy..............0 West Germany..............0 — Rome
B 8. 6. 74 Austria..............0 Italy..............0 — Vienna
C 15. 6. 74 Italy..............3 (Rivera, Benetti, Anastasi) Haiti..............1 (Sanon) — Munich (WC)
D 19. 6. 74 Italy..............1 (Perfumo o.g.) Argentina..............1 (Houseman) — Stuttgart (WC)
E 23. 6. 74 Italy..............1 (Capello) Poland..............2 (Szarmach, Deyna) — Stuttgart (WC)
F 28. 9. 74 Yugoslavia..............1 (Surjak) Italy..............0 — Zagreb
G 20. 11. 74 Netherlands..............3 (Rensenbrink, Cruyff 2) Italy..............1 (Boninsegna) — Rotterdam (EFC)

	A	B	C	D	E	F	G
Zoff	G	G	G	G	G	G	G
Spinosi	RB	RB	RB	RB	RB	—	—
Rocca	—	—	—	—	—	RB	RB
Benetti	RCB	RCB	RCB	RCB	RCB	RCB	—
Zecchini	—	—	—	—	—	RH	RCB
Wilson	LCB	—	—	RH[2]	LCB[2]	—	—
Burgnich	—	LCB	LCB	LCB	LCB[1]	—	—
Roggi	—	—	—	—	—	LCB	LB
Orlandini	—	—	—	—	—	—	LCB
Facchetti	LB[1]	LB	LB	LB	LB	LB	—
Sabadini	LB[2]	—	—	—	—	—	—
Morini	RH	RH	RH	RH[1]	RH	—	CH
Capello	CH[1]	CH	CH	CH	CH	CH	—
Rivera	LH	LH	LH	LH[1]	—	—	—
Causio	—	RF[2]	—	LH[2]	LH	—	RH
Re Cecconi	—	—	—	—	—	LH	—
Juliano	CH[2]	—	—	—	—	—	LH
Mazzola	RF	RF[1]	RF	RF	RF	—	—
Caso	—	—	—	—	—	RF[1]	—
Damiani	—	—	—	—	—	RF[2]	—
Antognoni	—	—	—	—	—	—	RF
Chinaglia	CF	CF[1]	CF[1]	—	CF[1]	—	—
Anastasi	—	CF[2]	CF[2]	CF	LF	—	LF
Boninsegna	—	LF	—	—	CF[2]	CF	CF
Chiaruggi	LF	—	—	—	—	—	—
Riva	—	—	LF	LF	—	—	—
Prati	—	—	—	—	—	LF	—

WALES

A 11. 5. 74 Wales..............0 England..............2 (Bowles, Keegan) — Cardiff (BHC)
B 14. 5. 74 Scotland..............2 (Dalglish, Jardine) Wales..............0 — Glasgow (BHC)
C 18. 5. 74 Wales..............1 (Smallman) N. Ireland..............0 — Wrexham (BHC)
D 4. 9. 74 Austria..............2 (Kreuz, Krankl) Wales..............1 (Griffiths) — Vienna (EFC)
E 30. 10. 74 Wales..............2 (Griffiths, Toshack) Hungary..............0 — Cardiff (EFC)
F 20. 11. 74 Wales..............5 (Toshack, England, P. Roberts, Griffiths, Yorath) Luxembourg..............0 — Swansea (EFC)

	A	B	C	D	E	F
J. Phillips	G	—	—	G[2]	—	—
Sprake	—	G	G	G[1]	G	G
P. Roberts	RB[1]	—	—	RB	RCB	RCB
Cartwright	RB[2]	LH	LH	—	—	—
Thomas	LB	RB	RB	—	RB	RB
J. Roberts	RCB	RCB	RCB	RCB	—	—
D. Roberts	LCB	LCB	—	LCB	—	—
Page	—	LB	LCB	—	—	—
England	—	—	—	—	LCB	LCB
L. Phillips	—	—	LB	LB	LB	LB

	A	B	C	D	E	F
Yorath	RH	CH	CH	CH	CH	CH
Mahoney	LH	RH	RH	RH	RH	RH[1]
Flynn	—	—	—	—	—	RH[2]
Villars	CH	RF	CF[2]	—	—	—
Griffiths	—	—	—	LH	LH	LH
Reece	RF	CF[1]	RF	RF	RF	RF
R. Davies	CF[1]	—	—	—	—	—
Smallman	CF[2]	CF[2]	CF[1]	—	—	—
Toshack	—	—	—	CF	CF	CF
James	LF	LF	LF	LF	LF	LF

NETHERLANDS

A 27. 3. 74 Netherlands.................1 (Krol) Austria.....................1 — Amsterdam (Krankl)

B 26. 5. 74 Netherlands.................4 (Neeskens, Strik, Rensenbrink, Haan) Argentina.................1 — Amsterdam (Wolff)

C 5. 6. 74 Netherlands.................0 Rumania...................0 — Rotterdam

D 15. 6. 74 Netherlands.................2 (Rep 2) Uruguay...................0 — Hanover (WC)

E 19. 6. 74 Netherlands.................0 Sweden....................0 — Dortmund (WC)

F 23. 6. 74 Netherlands.................4 (Neeskens 2, Rep, De Jong) Bulgaria..................1 — Dortmund (WC) (Krol o.g.)

G 26. 6. 74 Netherlands.................4 (Cruyff 2, Krol, Rep) Argentina.................0 — Gelsenkirchen (WC)

H 30. 6. 74 Netherlands.................2 (Neeskens, Rensenbrink) East Germany..............0 — Gelsenkirchen (WC)

I 3. 7. 74 Netherlands.................2 (Neeskens, Cruyff) Brazil....................0 — Dortmund (WC)

J 7. 7. 74 West Germany...............2 (Breitner, Muller) Netherlands...............1 — Munich (WC Final) (Neeskens)

K 4. 9. 74 Sweden....................1 (Larsson) Netherlands...............5 — Stockholm (Cruyff, Neeskens 3, Rensenbrink)

L 25. 9. 74 Finland....................1 (Rahja) Netherlands...............3 — Helsinki (EFC) (Cruyff 2, Neeskens)

M 9. 10. 74 Netherlands.................1 (Geels) Switzerland...............0 — Rotterdam

N 20. 11. 74 Netherlands.................3 (Rensenbrink, Cruyff 2) Italy.....................1 — Rotterdam (EFC) (Boninsegna)

	A*	B	C	D	E	F	G	H	I	J	K	L	M	N
Schrijvers	G	—	—	—	—	—	—	—	—	—	—	—	—	—
Jongbloed	—	G	—	G	G	G	G	G	G	G	G	G	G	G
Treytel	—	—	G	—	—	—	—	—	—	—	—	—	—	—
Van Iersel	RB	CH²	RH²	—	—	—	—	—	—	—	RB	—	CH²	—
Suurbier	—	RB	RB	RB	RB	RB	RB¹	RB	RB	RB	RB	—	RB	RB
Notten	RCB	—	—	—	—	—	—	—	—	—	CH²	—	CH¹	—
Strik	—	RCB	—	—	—	—	—	—	—	—	—	—	—	—
Haan	—	RH	LCB	RCB	RCB	RCB	RCB	RCB	RCB	RCB	RCB¹	LCB	RCB¹	RCB
Peters	—	—	—	—	—	—	—	—	—	—	RCB²	—	—	—
Schneider	—	—	—	—	—	—	—	—	—	—	LCB	—	RCB²	—
Dekker	LCB²	—	—	—	—	—	—	—	—	—	—	—	—	—
Israel	—	LCB	—	—	—	CH²	RB²	—	LH²	—	—	—	—	—
Rijsbergen	—	—	RCB²	LCB	LCB	LCB	LCB	LCB	LCB	LCB¹	—	—	—	LCB
Krol	LB	LB	LB	LB	LB	LB	LB	LB	LB	LB	LB	LB	LB	LB
De Jong	RH	—	LH	—	CH²	LH²	—	—	LF²	LCB²	RH	RCB	RH	—
Neeskens	LCB¹	CH¹	RH¹	LH	LH	LH¹	LH	LH	LH¹	LH	LH	LH	—	CH
Jansen	OR²	—	RCB¹	RH	RH	RH	RH	RH	RH	RH	—	RH	LCB	—
Van der Kuylen	—	—	—	—	—	—	—	—	—	—	—	—	—	RH
Van Hanegem	LH	LH	CH¹	CH	CH¹	CH¹	CH	CH	CH	CH	CH¹	CH	LH¹	LH
W. Van der Kerkhof	—	CH²	—	—	—	—	—	—	—	—	—	—	—	RF²
Rep	OR¹	RF¹	—	RF	RF	RF	RF	RF	RF	RF	RF¹	RF	—	RF¹
Geels	RCF	RF²	CF	—	—	—	—	—	—	—	—	—	CF	—
Ressel	—	—	—	—	—	—	—	—	—	—	RF²	LF	RF	—
Cruyff	LCF	CF	—	CF	CF	CF	CF	CF	CF	CF	CF	CF	—	CF
Rensenbrink	OL	LF	RF	LF	—	LF	LF	LF	LF¹	LF¹	LF	—	LF	LF
Keizer	—	—	LF¹	—	LF	—	—	—	—	—	—	—	—	—
R. Van der Kerkhof	—	LF²	—	—	—	—	—	—	—	LF²	—	—	—	—

*4–2–4

SCOTLAND

A	27. 3. 74	West Germany..............2 (Breitner, Grabowski)	Scotland....................1 (Dalglish)	—	Frankfurt
B	11. 5. 74	N. Ireland.................1 (Cassidy)	Scotland...................0	—	Glasgow (BHC) (N.I. 'home' match)
C	14. 5. 75	Scotland...................2 (Dalglish, Jardine)	Wales......................0	—	Glasgow (BHC)
D	18. 5. 74	Scotland...................2 (Pejic o.g., Todd o.g.)	England....................0	—	Glasgow (BHC)
E	1. 6. 74	Belgium....................2 (Hentoray, Lambert)	Scotland...................1 (Johnstone)	—	Brussels
F	6. 6. 74	Norway.....................1 (Lund)	Scotland...................2 (Jordan, Dalglish)	—	Oslo
G	14. 6. 74	Scotland...................2 (Lorimer, Jordan)	Zaire......................0	—	Dortmund (WC)
H	18. 6. 74	Scotland...................0	Brazil.....................0	—	Frankfurt (WC)
I	22. 6. 74	Scotland...................1 (Jordan)	Yugoslavia.................1 (Karasi)	—	Frankfurt (WC)
J	30. 10. 74	Scotland...................3 (Hutchison, Burns, Dalglish)	East Germany...............0	—	Glasgow
K	20. 11. 74	Scotland...................1 (Bremner)	Spain......................2 (Quini 2)	—	Glasgow (EFC)

	A	B	C	D	E	F	G	H*	I	J	K
Allan	G	—	—	—	—	G	—	—	—	—	—
Harvey	—	G	G	G	G	—	G	G	G	G	G
Jardine	RB	RB	RB	RB	RB	RB	RB	RB	RB	RB	RB
Schaedler	RCB	—	—	—	—	—	—	—	—	—	—
Holton	—	RCB	RCB	LCB	—	RCB	RCB	RCB	RCB	RCB[1]	—
Blackley	—	—	—	RCB	RCB	—	LCB	—	—	—	—
Burns	LH[1]	—	—	—	—	—	—	—	—	RCB[2]	LB
McQueen	—	—	—	—	LCB	—	—	—	—	—	RCB
Buchan	LCB	LCB	LCB	—	—	LCB	—	LCB	LCB	LCB	—
A. Forsyth	—	—	—	—	—	—	—	—	—	LB	LCB
Stanton	LB	—	—	—	—	—	—	—	—	—	—
Donachie	—	LB[1]	—	—	—	—	—	—	—	—	—
J. Smith	—	LB[2]	LH[2]	—	—	—	—	—	—	—	—
Hay	RH	LH	LB	LH	LH	LH	CH	LCH	RH	—	—
McGrain	—	—	—	LB	LB	LB	LB	LB	—	—	RH
Bremner	—	RH	RH	RH	RH	RH	RH	RCH	CH	—	RH
Souness	—	—	—	—	—	—	—	—	—	RH	CH
Morgan	CH	CH	—	—	CH[2]	—	—	RH	LH	—	—
Dalglish	RF	CF	CH	CH	CH[1]	CH[2]	LH[1]	LH	LF[1]	CH	LH[2]
J. Johnstone	—	—	RF	RF	RF[1]	CH[1]	—	—	—	LF	LF
Robinson	LH[2]	—	—	—	—	—	—	—	—	—	—
Hutchison	LF	LF	LH[1]	—	RF[2]	LF	LH[2]	—	LF[2]	LH	LH[1]
Law	CF[1]	RF[1]	—	—	—	—	LF	—	—	—	—
Jordan	—	RF[2]	LF	CF	CF	CF	CF	LF	CF	CF	CF
Lorimer	—	—	—	LF	LF	RF	RF	RF	RF	—	RF[2]
Deans	—	—	—	—	—	—	—	—	—	RF	RF[1]
Ford	CF[2]	—	CF	—	—	—	—	—	—	—	—

*4–4–2

SWEDEN

A	1. 5. 74	West Germany ....2 (Hoeness, Heynckes)	Sweden 0	— Hamburg
B	3. 6. 74	Denmark...................0	Sweden ....2 (Sandberg, Torstensson)	— Copenhagen
C	9. 6. 74	Sweden 0	Switzerland.................0	— Malmo
D	15. 6. 74	Sweden 0	Bulgaria....................0	— Dusseldorf (WC)
E	19. 6. 74	Sweden 0	Netherlands.................0	— Dortmund (WC)
F	23. 6. 74	Sweden ....3 (Edstrom 2, Sandberg)	Uruguay 0	— Dusseldorf (WC)
G	26. 6. 74	Sweden 0	Poland.....................1 (Lato)	— Stuttgart (WC)
H	30. 6. 74	West Germany ....4 (Overath, Bonhof, Grabowski, Hoeness)	Sweden ....2 (Edstrom, Sandberg)	— Dusseldorf (WC)
I	3. 7. 74	Sweden ....2 (Edstrom, Torstensson)	Yugoslavia..................1 (Surjak)	— Dusseldorf (WC)
J	8. 8. 74	Sweden ....2 (Fredriksson, Tapper)	Norway ....1 (Hestad)	— Gothenburg
K	4. 9. 74	Sweden ....1 (Bo Larsson)	Netherlands.................5 (Cruyff, Neeskens 3, Rensenbrink)	— Stockholm
L	13. 10. 74	Czechoslovakia..............4 (Svehlik 2, Masny, Bicovsky)	Sweden 0	— Bratislava
M	30. 10. 74	Sweden 0	N. Ireland..................2 (Nicholl, O'Neill)	— Stockholm (EFC)

	A	B	C	D	E	F	G	H	I	J	K	L	M
Hellstrom	G[1]	G	G	G	G	G	G	G	G	—	G	—	G
S-G. Larsson	G[2]	—	—	—	—	—	—	—	—	—	—	—	—
Gustavsson	—	—	—	—	—	—	—	—	—	G	—	G	—
Olsson	RB[1]	RB[1]	RB	RB	RB[1]	—	—	RB	RB	RB[1]	RB[2]	—	—
B. Andersson.....	LB	LB	LB	RCB	RCB	RB	RB[1]	—	—	—	LB	LB	LB
Augustsson	—	—	—	—	—	—	RB[2]	RCB	RCB	LB	—	—	—
Rol. Andersson...	—	—	—	—	—	—	—	—	—	RB[2]	RB[1]	RB	RB
Nordqvist	—	LCB	LCB[1]	—	LB	LB	LCB	LB	LB	—	—	—	LCB
Grip............	RB[2]	RB[2]	—	—	RB[2]	RCB	LB	—	—	—	—	—	—
Karlsson	RCB	—	LCB[2]	LCB	LCB	LCB	RCB	LCB	LCB	RCB	RCB	RCB	RCB
Bo Larsson.......	LCB	RCB	RCB	RH	RH	RH	RH	RH[1]	—	—	RH	—	CH
Cronqvist........	—	—	—	—	—	—	—	—	—	LCB	LCB	—	—
Lindman	—	—	LH[1]	—	—	—	—	—	—	CH	—	LCB[1]	—
Roy Andersson ...	—	—	—	—	—	—	—	—	—	—	—	LCB[2]	—
Tapper..........	RH	CH	CH	LB	LH[1]	—	LH[1]	LH	LH	RH	LH[1]	—	RH
Kindvall	LH[1]	RH	—	LH[1]	—	LH[1]	—	—	—	—	—	CH	LH[1]
Grahn	CH	—	RH	CH	CH	CH	CH	CH	CH	—	CH	—	—
Persson..........	LH[2]	LH	—	—	LH[2]	—	—	—	RH	—	—	—	—
Almquist	—	—	—	—	—	—	—	—	—	—	—	RH	—
Magnusson	—	—	LH[2]	LH[2]	—	RF[1]	—	—	—	—	RF[1]	—	—
Ahlstrom	CF[2]	—	—	—	—	LH[2]	LH[2]	—	—	LF	LF	RF[2]	—
Fredriksson	—	—	—	—	—	—	—	—	—	LH	—	—	—
Lundberg	—	—	—	—	—	—	—	—	—	—	LH[2]	LH	—
Torstensson......	RF	RF	RF	RF	—	RF[2]	RF	RF	RF	—	—	—	RF[1]
Ejderstedt	CF[1]	—	—	—	RF	—	—	RH[2]	—	RF[1]	—	—	—
Sjostrom	—	—	—	—	—	—	—	—	—	RF[2]	RF[2]	—	—
Leback..........	—	—	—	—	—	—	—	—	—	—	—	RF[1]	—
Mattsson	—	—	—	—	—	—	—	—	—	—	—	LF	RF[2]
Edstrom.........	—	CF	LF	CF	CF	CF	CF	CF	CF	—	—	—	CF
Sjoberg	—	—	—	—	—	—	—	—	—	CF	—	—	—
Nordahl.........	—	—	—	—	—	—	—	—	—	—	—	CF	LH[2]
Sandberg........	LF	LF	CF	LF	LF	LF	LF	LF	LF	—	CF	—	LF

YUGOSLAVIA

A 13. 2. 74 Yugoslavia.................1 Spain......................0 — Frankfurt (WC)
   (Katalinski)

B 17. 4. 74 Yugoslavia ....0 U.S.S.R...................1 — Belgrade
   (Kipiani)

C 29. 5. 74 Hungary...................3 Yugoslavia.................2 — Szekesfehervar
   (Mate 2, Fazekas) (Popivoda, Jerkovic)

D 5. 6. 74 Yugoslavia.................2 England....................2 — Belgrade
   (Petkovic, Oblak) (Channon, Keegan)

E 13. 6. 74 Yugoslavia.................0 Brazil.....................0 — Frankfurt (WC)

F 18. 6. 74 Yugoslavia.................9 Zaire......................0 — Gelseekirchen (WC)
   (Bajevic 3, Dzajic, Surjak, Katalinski, Bogicevic, Oblak, Petkovic)

G 22. 6. 74 Yugoslavia.................1 Scotland...................1 — Frankfurt (WC)
   (Karasi) (Jordan)

H 26. 6. 74 West Germany..............2 Yugoslavia.................0 — Dusseldorf (WC)
   (Breitner, Muller)

I 30. 6. 74 Yugoslavia.................1 Poland.....................2 — Frankfurt (WC)
   (Karasi) (Deyna, Lato)

J 3. 7. 74 Yugoslavia.................1 Sweden.....................2 — Dusseldorf (WC)
   (Surjak) (Edstrom, Torstensson)

K 28. 9. 74 Yugoslavia.................1 Italy......................0 — Zagreb
   (Surjak)

L 30. 10. 74 Yugoslavia.................3 Norway.....................1 — Belgrade (EFC)
   (Vukotic, Katalinski 2) (Lund)

	A	B	C	D	E	F*	G*	H	I	J	K	L
Maric	G	G	G	G	G	G	G	G	G	G	—	—
O. Petrovic	—	—	—	—	—	—	—	—	—	—	G	G
Buljan	RB	RB	RCB	RB	RB	RB	RB	RB	RB	RB	LB	RB
Krivokuca	—	—	RB¹	RCB¹	—	—	—	—	—	—	—	—
Hatunic	—	—	RB²	—	—	—	—	—	—	—	—	—
Bogicevic	RCB	RCB	—	LB	LCB	LCB	LCB	—	LCB	LCB	—	—
Katalinski	LCB	LCB	LCB	LCB	RCB	RCB	RCB	RCB	RCB	RCB	RCB	LCB
Djoni	—	—	—	—	—	—	—	—	—	—	RB	RCB
Muzinic	—	RH¹	RH	RH¹	RH	—	—	LCB	—	—	—	—
Hadziabdic	LB	LB¹	—	RCB²	LB	LB	LB	LB	LB	LB	LCB	LB
Pavlovic	—	—	LB	—	—	—	—	—	—	RH¹	—	—
Oblak	RH	—	—	CH	CH	RH	RH	RH¹	RH¹	—	RH	—
Holcer	—	RH²	—	—	—	—	—	—	—	—	—	—
Peruzovic	—	—	—	—	—	—	—	—	RH²	—	—	—
Jerkovic	—	CH	CH	—	—	—	LF²	RH²	CH	CH	—	RH
Karasi	CH	RF¹	—	—	—	—	LCF²	CH	CH	RF²	—	—
Zungul	—	—	—	—	—	—	—	—	—	—	RF²	CH
Acimovic	LH	LH	LH	LH	LH	LH	LH	LH	LH	LH	—	—
Vukotic	—	—	—	—	—	—	—	—	—	—	—	LH
Petkovic	RF	—	—	RF	RF	OR	OR	RH²	RF¹	—	—	—
Bjekovic	—	RF²	—	—	—	—	—	—	—	—	—	—
Popivoda	—	—	RF¹	—	—	—	RF	—	—	RF¹	—	—
V. Petrovic	—	LB²	RF²	—	—	—	—	RF²	RF¹	LH	—	—
Surjak	CF	CF	CF	CF	CF	RCF	RCF	CF	LF	CF	LF	RF
Bajevic	—	—	RH²	—	—	LCF	LCF¹	—	CF	—	—	—
Vladic	—	—	LF¹	—	—	—	—	—	—	—	CF	CF¹
Rajkovic	—	—	—	—	—	—	—	—	—	—	—	CF²
Dzajic	LF	—	LF¹	LF	LF	OL	OL	LF¹	—	LF	—	LF
Santrac	—	LF²	—	—	—	—	—	—	—	—	—	—
Bukal	—	—	LF²	—	—	—	—	—	—	—	—	—

*4–2–4

FRANCE

A 23. 3. 74 France....................1 Rumania...................0 — Paris
  (Bereta)
B 27. 4. 74 Czechoslovakia............3 France....................3 — Prague
  (Pivarnik, Bicovsky, Panenka) (Chiesa, Lacombe 2)
C 18. 5. 74 France....................0 Argentina................1 — Paris
  (Kempes)
D 7. 9. 74 Poland....................0 France....................2 — Wroclaw
  (Coste, Jodar)
E 12. 10. 74 Belgium..................2 France....................1 — Brussels (EFC)
  (Martens, Van der Elst) (Coste)
F 16. 11. 74 France...................2 East Germany.............2 — Paris (EFC)
  (Guillou, Gallice) (Sparwasser, Kreische)

	A	B	C	D	E	F		A	B	C	D	E	F
Bertrand-Demanes	G	G	—	G	—	G	Molitor	—	—	LH	—	—	—
Baratelli	—	—	G	—	G	—	Dalger	RF[1]	—	—	—	—	—
Vanucci	RB	RB	—	—	—	—	P. Revelli	RF[2]	—	—	RF[2]	—	—
Repellini	—	—	RB	—	—	—	Sarramagna	—	—	RF	—	—	—
Jodar	—	—	RCB[2]	RB	RB	RB	Giresse	—	—	—	RF[1]	—	—
Adams	RCB	RCB[1]	LCB	RCB	RCB	RCB	Coste	—	—	—	CF	RF	CF[1]
Merchadier	—	RCB[2]	RCB[1]	CH[2]	—	—	Soler	—	—	—	—	—	RF
Tresor	LCB	LCB	—	LCB	LCB	LCB	H. Revelli	CF[1]	—	—	—	—	—
Bracci	LB	LB	LB	LB	LB	LB	Berdoll	CF[2]	—	—	—	—	—
Michel	RH	CH	—	CH[1]	RH	RH[1]	Lacombe	—	CF	CF[1]	—	CF[1]	—
Huck	—	RH	RH	RH	LH	CH	Loubet	—	—	CF[2]	—	—	—
Synaeghel	—	—	—	—	—	RH[2]	Gallice	—	—	—	—	CF[2]	CF[2]
Chiesa	CH	LH	—	—	—	—	Bereta	LF	LF	LF	LF	LF	LF
Guillou	LH	RF	CH	LH	CH	LH							

SPAIN

A 13. 2. 74 Yugoslavia................1 Spain....................0 — Frankfurt (WC Qual.)
  (Katalinski)
B 23. 2. 74 Spain....................0 West Germany.............0 — Barcelona
  (Asensi)
C 25. 9. 74 Denmark...................1 Spain....................2 — Copenhagen (EFC)
  (Nygaard) (Claramunt, R. Martinez)
D 13. 10. 74 Argentina................1 Spain....................1 — Buenos Aires
  (Rogel) (Pirri)
E 20. 11. 74 Scotland.................1 Spain....................2 — Glasgow (EFC)
  (Bremner) (Quini 2)

	A	B	C	D	E		A	B	C	D	E
Iribar	G	G	G	G	G	Reano	—	—	CH[2]	—	—
Sol	RB	RB	RB	RB	RH[2]	Villar	—	—	—	—	CH
Castellanos	—	—	RH	RCB	RB	Soriano	—	—	—	CH	—
Benito	RCB	LCB	RCB	LCB	RCB	Marcial	RF[2]	LH	CF	—	—
J. Martinez	LCB	RCB[1]	LB	—	—	Planas	—	—	—	—	LH
Costas	—	RCB[2]	—	—	LCB	Amancio	RF[1]	—	—	—	—
Capon	—	LB	LCB	RH	LB	Galan	—	RF[2]	—	—	—
Uriarte	LB	—	—	—	—	Irureta	—	—	—	RF	—
Pirri	—	—	—	LB	—	Garate	CF	—	—	—	—
Juan Carlos	RH[1]	—	—	—	—	Quini	RH[2]	CF	LF	CF	CF
Claramunt	CH	RH	LH	LH	—	Valdez	LF	—	—	—	—
Miguel	—	—	—	—	RH[1]	Churruca	—	LF[1]	—	LF	—
Asensi	LH	CH	RF	—	—	Rexach	—	LF[2]	—	—	LF
R. Martinez	—	RF[1]	CH[1]	—	RF						